Mindboggling

Preliminaries to a science of the mind

Roy Harris

The Pantaneto Press

Luton

Published by The Pantaneto Press, First Floor, 3 Gordon Street,
Luton, Bedfordshire, LU1 2QP, UK

Printed and bound in Great Britain by
Biddles Ltd, King's Lynn, Norfolk

2008

ISBN 978-0-9549780-2-0

The Pantaneto Forum

Founded in 2000. *The Pantaneto Forum* is a quarterly web-
based journal, which aims to promote debate on how scientists
communicate, with particular emphasis on how such communication can be improved through education and a better philosophical understanding of science.

www.pantaneto.co.uk

Contents

	Preface	vii
1	The vulgar mind	1
2	The ghostly mind	7
3	The well-behaved mind	13
4	The other mind	19
5	The wilful mind	25
6	The computerized mind	31
7	The encoding mind	37
8	The silent mind	43
9	The linguistic mind	49
10	The mind demythologized	55
11	The mind located	61
12	The self-evident mind	67
13	The verbalized mind	73
14	The unconscious mind	79
15	The conscious mind	85
16	The self-conscious mind	91
17	The extraordinary mind	97
18	The tidy mind	103
19	The integrated mind	109
20	The cosmic mind	115
21	The collective mind	121
22	The primitive mind	127
23	The relative mind	133
24	The mind defined?	139
25	The mind reinstated	145
26	The mind reported	149
27	My mind	155
	References	161
	Index	169

Preface

You may think that 'Do you have a mind?' is either a badly formulated question or else an insult to your intelligence. This book sets out to convince you that it is neither, by presenting some of the main arguments for and against the existence of minds. These are arguments that need to be dealt with before there can be any question of constructing a 'science' of the mind (or, for that matter, of the brain, or of both).

'Do you have a mind?' may sound to some scientists like a question that only philosophers are likely to ask. There is some truth in this. But this book is not a potted history of philosophy of mind, nor of psychology. However, it raises certain issues that are basic to both enterprises, and especially to the question of whether the human mind falls within the province of the natural sciences at all.

Anyone who asks 'Do you have a mind?' invites the facile answer: 'It all depends on what you mean by *mind.*' But this is not a 'purely verbal' question, and cannot be settled any way you like just by opting for whatever definition you prefer. I shall try to show why not.

Another reaction that I confidently anticipate is: it is absurd to write a book on this subject, because anyone who can write (or read) a book (on anything) must by definition have a mind. But, I shall maintain, although 'having a mind' is inextricably bound up in various ways with 'having a language', it is simplistic to treat the latter as evidence for the former.

In setting out my case I shall try to avoid technical terminology as far as possible. This is not because my aim is to present a dumbed-down version of the issues for the benefit of scientists with no background in psychology or philosophy or linguistics, but because I believe that in many cases the technical terminology has actually served to obscure or confuse those issues. When I have occasion to discuss the claims of various authorities, I shall give exact references and verbatim quotations, in preference to reliance on paraphrasing their pronouncements. In order to avoid any suspicion of rigging the evidence, when a passage needs to be translated from some language other than English, I shall cite other people's translations, in preference to supplying my own. Although I comment on many views about the mind, and list a large number of bibliographical references at the end, I have not attempted to give an introduction even to the basic reading on the subject: that would have required far more space than I have allowed myself.

I do not disguise my own views about the mind, but I try not to insist on them. The aim is to enable readers to see clearly where they disagree with me and where they don't. I make no attempt to present an 'impartial' account of these issues. What I say is part of an intellectual autobiography, reflecting my own digestion of and reactions to ideas about the mind that I have encountered. My excuse for this 'autobiographical' approach is that it is more honest than any attempt at impartiality. Unlike Galileo before the Inquisition, I am not obliged to pretend that conflicting opinions are equally worthy of respect, or that there is an ultimate truth of the matter laid down in Holy Writ (or – the modern equivalent – about to be revealed in the scriptures of Science).

There is, of course, an argument of my own about the mind that I want to put forward, and I would not have written this book otherwise. But I think the book can be read with profit even if you come to the conclusion that my argument fails to convince you, and that a science of the mind can go ahead without me.

Each chapter deals with one particular 'boggle' about the mind. I try in each case to explain how it arises and what to make of it. In the end, 'Do I have a mind?' is a question that individuals must answer for themselves. My main concern is to distinguish between silly and sensible ways of understanding the question, and to explain why it is a question worth taking seriously. My own answer will be found in the final chapter.

R.H.
Oxford, January 2008

Chapter One: The vulgar mind

'Do you have a mind?' is a question with a long history. Ignore that history and you risk losing some valuable answers. But paying too much attention to the past would risk being led astray, because the history of the question is both confused and confusing.

Where, then, can one start? I propose to start from the question itself as presented here, 'Do you have a mind?': that is, a question formulated in English and addressed to readers whose acquaintance with English is sufficient to enable them to grasp the relevant vocabulary and syntax. If you have no such acquaintance, I assume you would not be reading this book anyway. However, even if you have, that does not necessarily mean you understand *what* the question asks. To clarify that issue is precisely what this book attempts to do.

Asking 'Do you have a mind?' sounds at first as if it were a parallel question to 'Do you have a body?' and, because of the parallel, philosophers have spent a great deal of effort on what they call the 'mind/body problem'. For reasons I shall come back to, I think that much of this effort has been a waste of time. But I mention it at the outset to sound a cautionary note.

Where did you get the idea that you even *might* have a mind? I suggest it came from one or both of two sources. One is whatever you might happen to have read about the mind. But even if you have never read anything on the subject, there remains the other source, which I will call for convenience 'vulgar mindspeak'.

I call it 'vulgar mindspeak' because it is the kind of language that serves what an Oxford philosopher once called 'our vulgar concept of mind' (Hampshire 1971: 20). By this I think he meant whatever concept of mind seems *prima facie* to underlie saying such things as 'He *thinks* that the government has broken its election pledges' or 'She has a very curious *idea* of racial discrimination.' Here the words *thinks* and *idea* are words that belong to the kind of vocabulary I would customarily use for everyday purposes in discussing my own beliefs and those of others. Along with it goes saying such things as the following. 1. When decisions are called for, one must 'make up one's mind'. 2. Things not to be forgotten or overlooked must be 'borne in mind'. 3. When we revise an opinion, we 'change our mind'. 4. When there is a difficult task to be done or a problem to be solved, one 'puts one's mind to it'. 5. Two people in complete agreement are 'of the same mind'.

There is a related verb *to mind*. Things you may be called upon to mind include the baby, the step, the consequences and your Ps and Qs.

Since it would be tedious to keep repeating 'the-kind-of-language-that-is-customarily-used...etc.', I am going to call it 'vulgar mindspeak'. Vulgar mindspeak allows one to talk, in short, as if there were no doubt whatever that all human beings had minds, and that minds were where most of human thinking was done. That is the basis of the 'vulgar concept of mind', and I think this is the concept of mind I started with, before I had seriously '*thought* about' it at all. As the last sentence shows, it is difficult to say anything whatsoever on the subject without invoking the terminology of vulgar mindspeak.

So the vulgar mindspeak answer to the vulgar mindspeak inquiry 'Do you have a mind?' will be an unhesitating 'Yes, of course I do!' (And that reply might well be accompanied by some such remark as 'How else would I understand the question?') Vulgar mindspeak is treated by most people as requiring no further justification, because the assumptions on which it is based are those of everyday common sense.

Unfortunately, that kind of reply is not likely to satisfy sceptics for very long, because vulgar mindspeak is on the face of it no more trustworthy than vulgar healthspeak or vulgar moneyspeak or vulgar moralityspeak, or any other kind of discourse which purportedly enshrines popular wisdom. People seem naturally inclined in all these fields to look for something more reliable as a basis for discussion. They look to doctors to correct misguided assumptions about health, to economists to improve their understanding of money, and to philosophers or religious leaders to sharpen their grasp of the differences between right and wrong.

Vulgar mindspeak, in short, is part and parcel of what linguists and philosophers commonly classify as 'ordinary language'. The appeal to what 'ordinary language' says, or rather allows one to say, is no longer as popular as once it was. Nevertheless, it still crops up in arguments about the mind, especially between philosophers. John Searle, for example, commenting on David Chalmers' book *The Conscious Mind* (Chalmers 1996), rejects Chalmers' interpretation of the words *pain*, *belief*, etc. with the brusque rebuttal:

As a native speaker of English, I know what these words mean, and there is no meaning of the word "pain," for example, where for every conscious pain in the world there must be a correlated nonconscious functional state which is also called "pain." On the standard dictionary definition, "pain" means unpleasant sensation, and that definition agrees with my usage as well as that of my fellow English speakers. (Searle 1997: 169)

Here Searle's appeal to ordinary language seems to me to rest on a linguistic myth that I shall describe in detail later, and I do not think we can get very far with questions about the mind by arguing in this way. No serious philosophical issue was ever settled by consulting a dictionary.

Vulgar mindspeak is the language of what is sometimes called 'presystematic' or 'commonsense intuitions' about the mind (Rosenthal 2005: 23); or sometimes the language of 'folk psychology', although the latter term is misleading if taken to imply that this involves a tacit *theory* of the mind (Bennett and Hacker 2003: 367-77). Statements like 'I think today is Friday' or 'She was afraid of the dark' are not *theoretical* statements of psychology, any more than 'It is raining' is a theoretical statement of meteorology.

In this respect vulgar mindspeak is to be distinguished from an altogether different mindspeak idiom, which I am tempted to call 'cognobabble', currently employed in many publications concerning the mind. Cognobabble does introduce theoretical terms, and many of them. It avoids the use of vulgar words such as *thought* and *idea*, preferring to speak of *mental states* and *mental representations*. In cognobabble, we also hear not of *beliefs* but of *propositional attitudes* and *intentional contents*. I mention this because in current discussions of the mind one striking feature is that the initial questions are formulated in vulgar mindspeak (to make them readily intelligible), and the answers given in cognobabble (which is often not). Here is a sample cognobabble sentence, which I take from an *Introduction to the Philosophy of Cognitive Science*:

> Now it may be that so very much is done by the synergetic dynamics of the body-environment system that the neural contributions are indeed best treated, at times, as just the application of simple forces to a complex but highly interanimated system whose intrinsic dynamics then carry most of the load. (Clark 2001: 133)

Translated into vulgar mindspeak, this says roughly: often the mind just gets your body started on a task, and the body does the rest.

Now one of the reasons for the proliferation of cognobabble is that doubts have been thrown on the credentials of vulgar mindspeak at a very basic level, for reasons that I shall summarize in the next two chapters. But before proceeding to do that, I need to point out that what I am calling 'vulgar mindspeak' relates to only one of three possible views of the mind.

These views crop up time and again in the history of Western philosophy. They are: (1) that mind is a cosmic agency, independent of matter, and operating in mysterious ways throughout the universe; (2) that only human beings (and perhaps a few other higher vertebrates) have minds; and (3) that human communities and subcommunities have a collective mind, over and above the minds of the individuals comprising them. So there are at least three kinds of mind or levels of mindspeak: 'cosmic mind', 'personal mind' and 'collective mind'.

Vulgar mindspeak in the main relates to the second of these, although it can be extended in certain cases to the third. This kind of extension (as when people speak of 'the female mind', or 'the adolescent mind', or 'the Chinese mind') is one about which I have grave reservations, because I doubt whether the collectivities in question (all females, all adolescents, or all Chinese) have the kind of commonality that makes it sensible to make generalizations about their 'mind'.

Vulgar mindspeak, then, is in the first instance about the personal mind. It sanctions saying of Bill Smith such things as 'He can't make up his mind', 'He has a lot on his mind' and 'He was in two minds'. It also licences talking about what Bill Smith's intentions are, what his opinions are, what his reasons are and what he remembers. What grounds I have for attributing specific intentions, opinions, reasons and recollections to Bill Smith are, of course, a different matter. But it is vulgar mindspeak that allows me to raise such matters in the first place. At the same time, it discourages me from attributing intentions, opinions, reasons, etc. to Mount Everest or to the fly crawling at this moment across the paper on my desk. So vulgar mindspeak is not an entirely open-ended form of discourse: it sets certain tacit limits to talk about the mind, at the same time as making available certain useful possibilities.

How far can you trust it? That is the first problem to be addressed.

Chapter Two: The ghostly mind

Modern scepticism about the mind, and about the validity of vulgar mindspeak, has two main sources. The first of these is the aftermath of the debate initiated in the 17th century by the French philosopher and mathematician René Descartes (1596-1650).

According to Descartes (*Principia Philosophiae*, 1644), the mind that human beings have (or, as he sometimes prefers to call it, the 'rational soul') is a special kind of substance, radically different from the substance found in material objects. The latter has extension in space as its principal property or essence. Mind, on the other hand, has thought as its principal property: it is 'thinking substance'.

By advancing this thesis Descartes created for himself at least two problems. One was how to make sense of the notion of an immaterial substance. The other was the problem of explaining how, in the human being, these two disparate kinds of substance were connected. (For the latter he proposed an obscure anatomical solution, holding that interaction between mind and matter somehow takes place in the pineal gland.)

Descartes regarded the human brain as part of the body, and the body as a machine. Animals, in his view, had bodies but no minds, and hence were incapable of reasoning. Descartes conceded that in some respects animals surpass the abilities of human beings, but maintained that this does not prove their superior intelligence.

It proves rather that they have no intelligence at all,
and that it is nature which acts in them according
to the disposition of their organs. In the same way
a clock, consisting only of wheels and springs, can
count the hours and measure time more accurately
than we can with all our wisdom [*prudence*]. (Descartes 1637: I.141)

Descartes' appeal to the clock analogy is both revealing
and potentially confusing. For, strictly speaking, a clock
does not 'count the hours': it is we who count the hours by
reference to the position of the hands on the clock. But this
is only possible if the clock has been accurately designed
and made by the clock-maker. In the case of animals and human beings, the clock-maker – for Descartes – is God. Descartes' view of the mind is based on a theological premise.

The Cartesian dichotomy nevertheless set the framework for subsequent debate about the status of the mind.
In this debate all possible positions were eventually taken
and even given names ('identity theory', 'interactionism', 'neutral monism', 'psycho-physical parallelism',
etc.) But all encountered difficulties and no clear consensus emerged. The general view among philosophers
now seems to be that 'no solution stands out as markedly
superior to the others' (Shaffer 1967: 345). My concern
here is not the history of this debate but the relation between Descartes' view and the vulgar concept of mind.

Descartes can be read as supporting the vulgar concept
of mind up to a point.

He proposed an absolute distinction between mind and
brain, and thus justified the existence of vulgar mindspeak,
since what the mind does is not to be equated with what the
brain does. But a strict Cartesian will draw the line at the
point where vulgar mindspeak would allow us to attribute
thoughts, intentions, comprehension, etc. to animals. Thus
it would be false, or misleading, to say that the dog who
sits when told to sit has 'understood' the command. The
sheep-dog who successfully rounds up the sheep by an

adroitly executed series of manoeuvres must not be said to have 'planned' the operation. The dog who brings along its lead and looks wistfully up at its owner must not be said to be 'expecting' or 'hoping' to be taken for a walk; even less to have brought the lead 'because' it wants to be taken for a walk. The dog wagging its tail excitedly at the sight of a new bone must not be described as 'happy'. And – perhaps most important of all – the dog who responds to its name must never be said to 'know what its name is' (that being a quasi-linguistic proficiency). Since understandings, intentions, hopes, expectations, decisions, reasons and emotional states are all mental phenomena, to credit a dog with these would be tantamount to implying that it had some kind of mind. In short, where the vulgar concept of the mind falls short, in the Cartesian view, is not only in its failure to treat the mind as a special kind of substance, thus leaving the connexion between mind and brain unexplained, but in being unpardonably lax about enforcing a rigid separation between human and non-human attributes.

The Cartesian position, according to its leading modern critic (Ryle 1949), rests on one huge mistake. It is the mistake of supposing that the mind is a kind of ghost housed inside a machine. This is the ghost alluded to in the title of this chapter. Descartes also thought, according to Ryle, that 'minds are not merely ghosts harnessed to machines, they are themselves just spectral machines' (Ryle 1949: 21).

Exorcising this kind of ghost is not a simple business, because the whole idiom of vulgar mindspeak, according to Ryle, is riddled with misunderstandings and misinterpretations that have led (almost all) philosophers astray. These mistakes cluster around familiar mindspeak terms such as *knowing, imagining, thinking, considering, meaning, guessing, recognizing*, etc., and have arisen through supposing that these words designate private mental acts.

> The verbs, nouns and adjectives, with which in ordinary life we describe the wits, characters and higher-grade performances of the people with whom we have to do, are

required to be construed as signifying special episodes
in their secret histories, or else as signifying tendencies
for such episodes to occur. When someone is described
as knowing, believing or guessing something, as hoping,
dreading, intending or shirking something, as designing
this or being amused at that, these verbs are supposed to
denote the occurrence of specific modifications in his (to
us) occult stream of consciousness. Only his own privi-
leged access to this stream in direct awareness and introspection could provide authentic testimony that these
mental-conduct verbs were correctly or incorrectly applied. (Ryle 1949: 16-17)

If Ryle is right, then vulgar mindspeak is not to be
trusted at all. Both Descartes and Ryle, however, have
been criticized for underestimating machines. The suggestion is that even a machine, if its internal structure is
sufficiently complex, can exhibit puzzling features which
seem to be beyond the capacity of mere nuts and bolts.
Richard Gregory, in his book *Mind in Science*, makes
this observation about clocks. It is the structure of the
clock which accounts for the fact that it can keep time:

if the parts were disassembled, lying around in a
box, there would be no time-keeping and no clock
but bits and pieces that could be assembled as a
clock. [...] This is as though, in Gilbert Ryle's famous phrase again, there is a ghost in the machine,
which lurks among the pieces that we can see, and
which is incarnated when the pieces are assembled
as a clock. (Gregory 1981: 86)

The point is that the clock has no single component responsible for keeping time. Nevertheless, the whole clock
in working order can function as a chronometer. Now
the human brain is structurally far more complex than a
clock. So – the implication is – we cannot dismiss out of
hand the possibility that its mental capacities are a func-

tion of that complexity. In that case, there is no need to postulate, with Descartes, a special 'thinking substance', and no need to go ghost-hunting with Ryle either. Vulgar mindspeak is in order just as it is, provided we realize that what its terms refer to are not the mechanical workings of the brain itself, but what these complex workings allow possessors of human brains to do with them.

Whether appeal to the 'complexity' factor clears up the mystery of the mind is a question I shall come back to shortly.

Chapter Three: The well-behaved mind

The other principal source of doubts about the mind and vulgar mindspeak can be traced to the advent of behaviourism in psychology. This emerged in 1912, according to J.B. Watson, one of the founding fathers of the movement. At about that time, he claimed, psychologists began to realize that 'consciousness is neither a definite nor a usable concept' and that 'belief in consciousness goes back to the ancient days of superstition and magic' Watson 1924: 2). In Watson's opinion, 'the great mass of the people' in his own day had 'not yet progressed very far away from savagery'.

> Almost every era has its new magic, black or white, and its new magician. Moses had his magic: he smote the rock and water gushed out. Christ had his magic: he turned water into wine and raised the dead to life. Coué had his magic word formula. Mrs. Eddy had a similar one.
>
> Magic lives forever. As time goes on, all of these critically undigested, innumerably told tales get woven into the folk lore of the people. Folk lore in turn gets organized into religions. Religions get caught up into the political and economic network of the country. Then they are used as tools. The public is forced to accept all the old wives' tales, and it passes them on as gospel to its children's children. (Watson 1924: 2)

Belief in the mind, if Watson was right, is just part

and parcel of this culturally transmitted 'gospel'. Along
with the rejection of consciousness as the subject matter of psychology went the dismissal of the mind as the
supposed seat of consciousness. It was surplus to requirements. The requirements in question were those of what
Watson and his colleagues called 'scientific psychology'.

Scientific method, on their view, demanded objective
and independently verifiable evidence. The trouble with
consciousness was that it was directly accessible only
subjectively, i.e. by introspection. There was no possibility of anyone else checking one's own introspections.
Behaviour, on the other hand, was available to observation in the same way as demanded by other sciences
(physics, chemistry, geology, etc.). Eliminating the mind
was therefore seen as an essential step in an academic
programme that aimed at making psychology a science.

B.F. Skinner, generally regarded one of the leading behaviourists of the second half of the 20th century, drew
a distinction between 'methodological' behaviourists and
'radical' behaviourists. Methodological behaviourists are
willing to accept the existence of feelings and states of
mind, but ignore them 'because they are not public and
hence statements about them are not subject to confirmation by more than one person.' Radical behaviourists, on
the other hand, contend that 'so-called mental activities are
metaphors or explanatory fictions' and that what is attributed to them in human behaviour can be 'more effectively
explained in other ways' (Skinner 1987: 74). By Skinner's
criteria, Watson counts as a radical behaviourist from the
start, since he explicitly refers to 'the fiction that there
is any such thing as "mental" life' (Watson 1924: 224).

For Watson, therefore, mindspeak is to be condemned *in toto* as 'unscientific'. It appears indeed
to be the principal means by which the 'gospel' of
mind is passed on to generation after generation.

Watson's rejection of mindspeak was endorsed by
one of the leading linguistic theorists of the interwar period, Leonard Bloomfield, who waged an unending strug-

gle against what he called 'mentalism' (or sometimes 'animism') in linguistics. Was Bloomfield a 'radical' or merely a 'methodological' behaviourist? Sometimes he sounds like the latter, as when, for instance, he claims:

> In the division of scientific labor, the linguist deals only with the speech-signal [...]; he is not competent to deal with problems of physiology or psychology. The findings of the linguist, who studies the speech-signal, will be all the more valuable for the psychologist if they are not distorted by any prepossessions about psychology. We have seen that many of the older linguists ignored this; they vitiated or skimped their reports by trying to state everything in terms of some psychological theory. (Bloomfield 1935: 32)

The historical irony in this is that Bloomfield proceeded to do exactly what he condemned his predecessors for doing, since he based his own linguistics on the psychological theory of Watson. But elsewhere Bloomfield's anti-mentalism seems more than just 'methodological': he condemns in general the use of such terms as *mind*, *consciousness*, *perception*, and *idea*, prophesying that eventually they will be discarded, 'much as we have discarded Ptolemaic astronomy' (Bloomfield 1936: 220). He also suggests that what underlies such notions as 'will', 'wish' and 'desire' is the fact that we can say in advance what the outcome of certain courses of action will be, and this leads us to suppose that such actions must be preceded by some silent announcement of this kind 'in the mind' (Bloomfield 1930: 152). Here he comes close to endorsing Watson's famous claim that 'what the psychologists have hitherto called thought is in short nothing but talking to ourselves' (Watson 1924: 238).

The term *mentalism* (and the implied rejection of behaviourism) is nowadays associated in linguistics primarily with the theorizing of Noam Chomsky, for whom 'linguistic theory is mentalistic, since it is concerned

with discovering a mental reality underlying actual behavior' (Chomsky 1965: 4). Chomsky, however, is quick
to hedge his bets about the nature of 'mental reality':

> The mentalist, in this traditional sense, need make no as-
> sumptions about the possible physiological basis for the
> mental reality that he studies. In particular, he need not
> deny that there is such a basis. (Chomsky 1965: 193)

So the Chomskyan mentalist is in the enviable position of being able to have it any way he likes, for it is no
concern of his *qua* linguist whether there is a further layer
of physical reality which underlies and explains the mental reality on which he has chosen to focus. (It is ironic
that on the same page Chomsky takes behaviourists to task
for concerning themselves exclusively with behaviour,
and their 'lack of interest' in explaining it. This is to assume that they are all just 'methodological' behaviourists.
On the other hand, the linguist's lack of interest in what
underlies mental reality is treated as perfectly reasonable.) In short, Chomskyan 'mental reality' emerges as no
more than one arbitrarily delimited level of 'description'
at which linguistic 'data' can be systematized. Whether it
captures any kind of reality at all is left as an unanswered
and perhaps unanswerable question, but this is no bar to
the endless proliferation of 'grammars' purporting to dis-
play it. (In any other academic enterprise than linguistics,
this would be called a licence to print your own money.)

For Chomskyans, therefore, an important part of the
linguist's concern is with the 'mental representations'
of linguistic items, but these 'representations' may be
'relatively abstract – i.e., not related in a simple way
to actual specimens of linguistic behavior' (Chomsky
1986: 43). For radical behaviourists, these supposed
mental representations would be just another 'fiction'.

We sometimes hear nowadays of *neuronal behaviourism* and *neuro-behaviourism*. These cognobabble terms
designate an approach deliberately 'excluding unobserva-

bles such as mental states but allowing publicly testable empirical data about nerve cells' (Rose 2006: 60). This fits the current materialist assumptions that prevail in empirical work on the brain. As Rose observes, 'it seems less controversial to say that one nerve cell causes another to fire than to say that one thought causes another thought' (Rose 2006: 61). But whether 'causation' is any better understood in the behaviour of nerve cells than in sequences of thoughts is, to say the least, open to question.

We also hear of *philosophical behaviourism*. This is described as 'the claim that for a system to have mental states of any kind is just a matter of its behaving or being disposed to behave, or capable of behaving, in certain ways' (Kirk 2005 : 204). This is supposed to let behaviourists off the awkward hook of having to say exactly *which* kind of behaviour or disposition corresponds to any given mental state. But it then becomes difficult to see how to draw the line between 'systems' that have mental states and those that do not. A system that has a reliable disposition to grow acorns is commonly known as an oak tree. Here philosophical behaviourism seems to merge with what might be called 'cosmic behaviourism'. (I shall return to the cosmic mind in Chapter Twenty.)

Chapter Four: The other mind

Thinking that you have a mind is one thing, but thinking that, for all you know, nothing *else* exists is quite another. If you belong in the latter category, you are what philosophers classify as a 'solipsist'. Various types of solipsist can be distinguished (called 'ontological solipsists', 'epistemological solipsists' and so on), but I shall not go into these niceties. If you are a solipsist of any kind, 'ideas' are just about the only things you have to worry about, and I shall leave you to it.

Nor shall I say anything about the 'idealism' associated with the Irish philosopher and Anglican bishop George Berkeley (1683-1753), who claimed that the material world would not exist if there were no mind to perceive it. When Boswell maintained that it was impossible to refute Berkeley's claim, Samuel Johnson 'striking his foot with mighty force against a large stone, till he rebounded from it, answered, "I refute it *thus*"'. Whether Johnson *had* refuted Berkeley, again I leave to you to decide.

The reason why I shall not go into these matters is that I think that if you have any solipsistic or Berkeleyan tendencies you probably suffer from a deep fear – possibly pathological – of being deceived by your own senses, but would like to pass this off as a rational conviction that the material world is illusory. There is nothing a book like this can do for you. Nor can it if, like some philosophers, you have bemused yourself into believing that consciousness must be a "mirage" (Hofstadter 2007: xii). Other minds are then just part of your personal mirage.

However, there are less severe forms of this psychological virus. Descartes was suffering from one when he produced the famous mentalistic argument 'I think: therefore I am' (*cogito ergo sum*). He might just as well have argued 'I sneeze: therefore I am'. If your sneezing might be illusory, so might your thinking; but not necessarily *your* illusion.

If you think you have a mind, but not the only mind in the business, it must occur to you to wonder whether you can know anything reliable about what is going on in these other minds. Some philosophers have made a great song-and-dance about this and called it 'the problem of other minds'.

One of the reasons for doubt is that we know people can lie. So we cannot take what they *say* they think as altogether reliable evidence. We also know that people can fake behaviour: so if Alice takes an aspirin, complaining of a headache, it may be that she is just trying to get out of keeping an appointment and has no headache at all.

This has led some philosophers to spend a great deal of time puzzling over words like *pain*, which seemingly refer to experiences that are essentially private. The usual assumption here is that I am the only ultimate authority for saying whether or not I am in pain, because nobody else can feel my pain anyway. It is as if I had a private bank account, to which no one else – not even the bank – had access: so I alone knew how much money was in it. But, as others have argued, this does not mean that no one else *could* know what is in the account: if that were so, all my cheques would bounce.

There seems to be an especially puzzling problem over cases where *thinking* that something is so seems actually to *make* it so. (This is different from the private bank account, where thinking I have a hundred pounds in it does not ensure that there is a hundred pounds in it.) Thus if I think that Smith has insulted me, it may be no use for Smith to protest that he has done nothing of the kind; for if

I (honestly) think I have been insulted, and I *do* feel insulted, nothing Smith can say by way of exculpation makes
any difference. I can perhaps agree that Smith did not *realize* he was insulting me; but he insulted me all the same.
Such cases may even be of international importance, as
shown by the case of Salman Rushdie and *The Satanic
Verses*. There just is no 'impartial' or 'neutral' point of
view from which it is possible to give a definitive judgment on whether *The Satanic Verses* is/was a blasphemous
text or not.

Unfortunately, this admission seems to let the case of
private experiences like pain back straight away into the
arena of dispute. If Jones honestly *believes* he is in pain,
is there any way he could be mistaken? He could be mistaken about the cause of the pain, but can he be mistaken,
for instance, about where it hurts? Doctors talk of 'referred
pain' when the pain that the patient thinks is located in one
place has its physiological source in another place. But
nevertheless, however mistaken Jones' personal diagnosis
of what is amiss may be, it seems hard to dispute that if he
is sure his ankle hurts, then it does hurt, even though it can
be shown that there is 'nothing wrong with it'. It would
be absurd to insist that Jones ought to be saying, e.g. 'My
ankle seems to hurt, but I can't be sure' or even 'The ankle
in my mind hurts'.

Psychologists too have made a fuss about 'other minds',
claiming that a child must acquire a 'theory' of the mind
and other minds in order to take part in games of make-
believe and other types of interaction which involve im-
aginatively 'putting oneself in someone else's place'. To
call this acquiring a 'theory' is piling one psychological
implausibility on top of another. For presumably the only
way a psychologist could 'know' that the child has constructed a *theory* is by extrapolating from the psychologist's own theorizing. But the problem of 'other minds'
is not solved by boldly foisting the concept on to the very
cases in which it is problematic. To play games of make-
believe, you do not need a theory of make-believe. One

might as well argue from a spider's ability to construct a web that it must somehow have (either innately or as a product of experimental learning) a theory of web structure. Make this claim on behalf of spiders if you wish; but I would say you are just anthropomorphizing (and devaluing the word *theory* into the bargain).

The crux of most philosophers' agitations about the problem of other minds is that they doubt whether it is sufficient to explain talk about someone else's private experience as being grounded in *analogy* with talk about our own private experience. The facile lay explanation is that we understand what Alice is claiming when she says she has a headache 'by analogy with' our own case when we have a headache. But then it seems that mere analogy can *never* give us an assurance that this is what Alice 'really' means, or that she may not be deceiving us. Quite so. But it was foolish to expect any such assurance in the first place.

This is related to what philosophers nowadays call the problem of 'qualia'. It might be pinpointed as follows:

> It would seem that the following situation is perfectly conceivable: When you look at a ripe tomato, your color experience is like the color I experience when I look at a bunch of spinach, and vice versa. That is, your experience of red might be qualitatively like my experience of green, and your experience of green is like my experience of red. These differences need not show up in any observable behavioral differences: We both say "red" when we are asked what color ripe tomatoes are, and we both describe the color of spinach as "green"; we are equally good at picking tomatoes out of mounds of lettuce leaves. (Kim 2006: 162)

The situation described by Kim differs from cases of so-called 'colour-blindness', where a person is unable to distinguish one colour from another. Here, the colours are distinguished by both viewers, but do not correspond to the same subjective experience. In short, where colour vision is concerned, your qualia may differ from my qualia. The 'contents' of our minds may differ and we would never know.

I find it difficult to get very worked up over this philosophical problem. It seems to me quite probable that your colour vision is rather different from mine (although unlikely to be as dissimilar as the 'qualia inversion' described above). Vulgar mindspeak can be applied unproblematically up to a point, but it cannot be pressed to yield results that exceed its own limitations. The fact is that it does not licence the claim that you are seeing my colours, or having my thoughts, any more than it licenses the claim that you are having my headache. Given those limitations, it is foolish to complain that there is no way of knowing what goes on in someone else's mind, as if that ought in some way to be comparable to knowing what goes on in your own.

Chapter Five: The wilful mind

The mind is popularly supposed to be the seat of the will, and the will is what enables us to make our own decisions. A long line of philosophers and theologians have taught us that Nature or God gave us 'free will', and that is what makes us responsible for our own actions and, at the same time, makes it wrong for others to force us to do what is against our will. So here morality enters directly into the realm of mindspeak.

Both philosophers and psychologists talk of 'will power' and 'akrasia' (i.e. weakness of the will, as when we succumb to temptation). New-age gurus and innumerable 'faith healers' propagate the facile doctrine that all cures are to be sought in the power of 'mind over matter' (to which, it goes without saying, they alone hold the key). Some philosophers – going back as far as Socrates – have found it problematic to explain how we can ever decide to act against our better judgment. But this is still a *mental* problem: no one supposes that the explanation lies in the neurophysiology of brain functions.

In his *Nichomachean Ethics* (Book III), Aristotle discusses the question of whether actions carried out when in certain mental states – e.g. in fear or when under compulsion – are *voluntary* or *involuntary*. For example, if a tyrant who threatened to kill your parents or your children ordered you to do something base in order to save their lives, would your decision to comply with his wishes be voluntary or not? Or if a ship is caught in a storm and valuable goods have to be thrown into the sea in order to secure the safety of the vessel and all those on board, is this course of action voluntary or involuntary? Aristotle reaches the conclusion that terms like voluntary and involuntary 'must be used with reference to the moment of action'. Thus although no one would choose to do a base act 'in the abstract', or throw away valuable goods, circumstances may arise in which the decision is rightly taken to follow those courses of action.

Determinists and fatalists hold all these dilemmas to be illusory and deny that the will has the freedom commonly attributed to it. The figure of Professor Godbole in the film of E.M. Forster's *A Passage to India* probably epitomises popular conceptions of what a fatalist believes. Godbole, a Brahman, does not deny that it is our responsibility to make up our minds about what to do, but he thinks that whatever we decide will in the end make no difference to the outcome, which has already been settled in advance. So in one sense we do have a choice, but that choice does not have the importance we usually attribute to it. It exercises no influence on what actually happens.

G.E. Moore tried to construct a theory of ethics which sidetracked the question of whether 'we do really have a choice' and started instead from defining 'voluntary' actions as those of which it is true that 'a particular act of will, just before their occurrence, would have been sufficient to *prevent* them' (Moore 1912: 10-11. Italics in the original). But here again discussion of ethical issues cannot get started without presupposing the 'reality' of acts of will.

For many people it goes against 'common sense' to deny that they can freely decide e.g. whether or not to give up their seat in a bus to an elderly person, or contribute a donation to charity (supposing they have the money to give). There may be considerations to be weighed on either side of so doing, but nevertheless – it is held – the ultimate decision itself, whichever way it goes, is surely a free act of the will, whether we decide to follow a certain course of action or to abstain from it.

According to Bertrand Russell, there is 'a sense in which will is an observable phenomenon, and another in which it is a metaphysical superstition' (Russell 1927: 231). The former is illustrated by saying 'I will hold my breath for thirty seconds' and proceeding to do so, while the latter consists in treating the will as an independent faculty or force. Russell approved of William James' view that 'a voluntary movement is merely one which is preceded by the thought of it, and has the thought of it as an essential part of its cause' (Russell 1927: 231). Russell concluded that 'there is nothing at all mysterious about the will', since 'whenever we think of a possible movement, we have a tendency to perform it, and are only restrained, if at all, by some thought, or other circumstance, having a contrary tendency' (Russell 1927: 232).

Others, however, have argued that the mistake here consists precisely in misconstruing decisions as causes in a causal chain. Thus a selfless act does not consist of two parts, viz. (i) a selfless decision that brings about (ii) a subsequent implementation having the quality of the prior decision that prompted it; rather, selflessness is just a characteristic of selfless acts. Ryle gives a typically sardonic analysis of 'frowning intentionally':

> To frown intentionally is not to do one thing on one's forehead and another thing in a second metaphorical place; nor is it to do one thing with one's brow-muscles and another thing with some non-bodily organ. In particular, it is not to bring about a frown on one's forehead by first bringing about a frown-causing exertion of some occult non-muscle. 'He frowned intentionally' does not report the occurrence of two episodes. It reports the occurrence of one episode, but one of a very different character from that reported by 'he frowned involuntarily', though the frowns might be photographically as similar as you please. (Ryle 1949: 72)

Determinists have often supposed that there is no room for free will if it is true that all our physical actions have determinate physical causes. But it can also be argued that there is no conflict:

> A complete physical explanation, showing how an action was determined by physical causes, would rule out determination by thought and decision only if these latter were some kind of external agencies that had to force their way into the chain-mesh of physical causes in the brain. If, however, our conscious thinking and deciding were embodied in the workings of our brains, in the sense in which an equation is *embodied in* those of a computer, there would be no contradiction in saying that our behaviour was determined by our thinking and choosing [...].
> (MacKay 1987: 190. Italics in the original.)

The two questions I shall focus on here are the following. First, do the subjective experiences I recognize when I make what seem to me to be freely willed decisions and choices constitute in themselves empirical evidence for the proposition that I have a mind? The answer to this has to be 'no', since it is conceivable that what I take to be my own deliberate decisions and choices are actually triggered by unconscious bodily processes and conditions of which I am not aware and which I cannot control.

Second, if this is so, then does not all talk of acts of the will, of decisions, personal commitment, my determination to carry out certain courses of action, etc. merely set up a linguistic smokescreen behind which the 'real' mechanisms involved are hidden? Should not this kind of talk therefore be banished from any sanitized mindspeak, or at least be disregarded?

That would be one conclusion. But there is another. It can be argued that if we can never be sure whether, as Moore puts, 'we really do have a choice' (i.e. of the voluntary kind that we *think* we do), then it is all the more essential that we retain a mindspeak that allows us to describe such experiences as trying to give up smoking, or hesitating about whether to hand in our resignation, and hundreds of others where *prima facie* the will is involved. For there simply is no other vocabulary that is currently available for such purposes. The option is not between retaining the traditional language of mental acts and substituting for it a more accurate mode of description. The alternatives are retaining the traditional language of mental acts or saying nothing at all, i.e. refusing to discuss those aspects of our human experience. And, paradoxically, opting for refusal looks on the face of it suspiciously like yet another act of free will.

Chapter Six: The computerized mind

Could your mind be a neural computer program installed in your head? This is currently the favourite hypothesis in 'cognitive science'. Most of the alleged evidence comes from language. Its background is research in artificial intelligence (AI). According to the version known as 'strong AI', there is nothing essentially biological about minds: 'the brain is just a digital computer and the mind is just a computer program' (Searle 1989: 28).

Descartes, in the pre-computer era, would never have thought of that. But he is in part responsible. Descartes held that linguistic abilities were the hallmark of the human mind. He argued that however cleverly an automaton might be constructed to resemble a human being, what would give it away would be its inability to answer questions. Such machines

> could never use words, or put together other signs, as we do in order to declare our thought to others. For we can certainly conceive of a machine so constructed that it utters words, and even utters words which correspond to bodily actions causing a change in its organs (e.g. if you touch it in one spot it asks what you want of it, if you touch it in another it cries out that you are hurting it, and so on). But it is not conceivable that such a machine should produce different arrangements of words so as to give an appropriately meaningful answer to whatever is

said in its presence, as the dullest of men can do. (Descartes 1637: 140)

Descartes' imaginary automaton was the ancestor of what philosophers nowadays call 'zombies': hypothetical creatures that are physiologically indistinguishable from human beings, but lack sentience and consciousness altogether (Kirk 2005). There is no *logical* impossibility – so it is claimed – in the existence of such creatures, and this shows that consciousness must be something of a different order from any physical set of properties. (Unrepentant materialists disagree.)

Long before zombies came on the scene, Descartes' challenge was taken up by the British mathematician Alan Turing in a celebrated paper entitled 'Computing machinery and intelligence' (Turing 1950). Turing directly addressed the question 'Can machines think?' and argued that if a machine can do what Descartes had declared an impossibility, namely answer questions, then there is no reason to deny that it can think.

Turing was confident that, at least in certain areas of discourse, machines could produce verbal performances indistinguishable from those of human beings. This confidence was based on the immense strides then being taken in the development of digital computers and robots. The 'Turing test', as it came to be called, is still going strong as an adjudicated international competition. Its most well-known non-verbal counterpart was the race to build a machine that could 'play chess'. This latter goal has now been reached, and we have a machine that can play and beat grand masters. It 'works' by having a computer program that can calculate enormous numbers of possible moves in advance and select the most advantageous. Something similar can be applied to a program for allowing a machine to take part in simple 'conversations'.

But what does all this tell us about the human mind? If Descartes were alive today, he would probably be surprised by what computers can do, but philosophically unmoved. He would argue, I suspect, as follows: 'God has allowed human beings to construct these marvellous machines that can out-perform human beings; but these man-made contrivances still have no minds, because God alone can create thinking substance. What machines (or animals) can *do* is not the ultimate test: the ultimate test is whether they *know what they are doing*.'

A similar line of thinking underlies another argument much debated in recent years. Advanced originally by the American philosopher John Searle, it is known as the 'Chinese room' argument. Searle challenges the view that sheer complexity of the processes involved could produce a mental activity out of mindless operations.

I shall quote the presentation of the 'Chinese room' argument that Searle gave in his 1984 Reith Lectures (a shorter version appears in Searle 2004) . He invites us to

> imagine that you are locked in a room, and in this room are several baskets full of Chinese symbols. Imagine that you (like me) do not understand a word of Chinese, but that you are given a rule book in English for manipulating these Chinese symbols. These rules specify the manipulations of the symbols purely formally, in terms of their syntax, not their semantics. So the rule might say: 'Take a squiggle-squiggle sign out of basket number one and put it next to a squoggle-squoggle sign from basket number two.' Now suppose that some other Chinese symbols are passed into the room, and that you are given further rules for passing back Chinese symbols out of the room. Suppose that unknown to you the symbols passed into the room are called 'questions' by the people outside the room, and the symbols you pass back out of the room are called 'answers to the questions'. Suppose, furthermore, that the programmers are so good at designing the programs and that you are so good at manipulating the symbols, that very soon your answers are indistinguishable from those of a native Chinese speaker. There you are locked in your room shuffling your Chinese symbols

and passing out Chinese symbols in response to incom-
ing Chinese symbols. On the basis of the situation as I
have described it, there is no way you could learn any
Chinese simply by manipulating these formal symbols.
(Searle 1989: 32)

This is, in effect, a Turing test in Chinese, and what
Searle is trying to demonstrate is that in order to pass
it a machine (or a human being operating a suitably
programmed machine) need not know any Chinese at
all. Unfortunately, the argument has an Achilles' heel.
It already presupposes that linguistic activities, such as
asking and answering questions, can be neatly divided
into a meaningful part and a meaningless part. But this
is extremely doubtful. According to Searle, there is no
way that the person in the Chinese room 'could learn any
Chinese simply by manipulating these formal symbols'.
Is this true? Using the rules requires matching up the
symbols, so it seems likely that eventually you would
become familiar with quite a number of symbols and
symbol sequences. If you got good enough at manipulating the symbols to dispense with looking up the rules
every time, you would have learnt quite a lot about their
concatenations. Searle's demonstration is based on the
assumption (no longer accepted by most linguists) that
syntax has nothing to do with meaning. The claim that
in the Chinese room you would be unable to learn any
Chinese is simply false. Familiarity with the characters
and some of the syntactic patterns is an indispensable part
of learning to read Chinese. Of course, in the Chinese
room you might not know that *what* you were learning
to handle was Chinese syntax, or even that these squig-
gles *were* Chinese characters. The same scenario could
be acted out on the basis of nonsense symbols. But that
is a different point from the one Searle is trying to prove,
which is that computers can handle only the meaningless
part of language.

There are in any case mental operations going on inside

the Chinese room: those involved in understanding the instructions and matching the symbols.

Searle's thought-experiment is aimed at the wrong target. The issue as regards strong AI is not about whether a computer could actually *learn*, simply by running it, whatever is instantiated in its program. What matters is whether it can operate effectively within the constraints of the program it is given and the communication system of which it is part. Searle's point seems to be that what goes on inside the Chinese room only 'simulates' an understanding of Chinese, without any 'real' understanding of the language being involved at all.

But this begs an important question about understanding. As Richard Gregory points out in his reply to Searle, you can say if you like that an automatic pilot only simulates what a human pilot does. But regardless of what you say, the fact remains that when the automatic pilot is in control 'it *actually* flies the plane' (Gregory 1987: 242). Analogously, the system set up in the Chinese room does not just simulate answering Chinese questions: it actually produces Chinese answers.

There is also a deeper linguistic fallacy involved in the Chinese room argument, to which I turn in the next chapter. I shall try to show how it throws doubt on Descartes' position on the mind as well as Searle's.

Chapter Seven: The encoding mind

To what extent does your view of the mind depend on your view of language? Far more, I suspect, than you realize or would be prepared to admit. You are in good company. It has so far escaped the attention of most philosophers and psychologists that although Descartes and Watson took very different views of the mind, they share a common basis. This common basis lies in what vulgar mindspeak allows us to say about words.

Words are commonly said to express 'thoughts' or 'ideas'. You put your thoughts into words either for your own satisfaction or in order to communicate these thoughts to others. You have to do this – the assumption is – because human beings (or the great majority of them) are not telepathic. A cannot get a message across to B just by an effort of sheer mental concentration. If the message is that B's father is ill, or that certain shares on the stock market are about to fall – or indeed any other message of any complexity, whether expected or unexpected – A's most reliable way of doing this is to express it verbally in words that B will understand. Words, in short, function as intermediaries or vehicles in the process of what I shall call thought-transference or 'telementation'. The essential difference between telepathy and telementation is that the latter requires (whereas the former does not) the production of a material sign of some kind. Words are, precisely, such signs. They come in two main varieties. The audi-

ble variety we call 'speech' and the visible variety we call
'writing'. Both varieties enable the same thoughts to be
expressed: an e-mail saying 'Your father is ill' conveys
the same message as a telephone call using the same four
words.

Telementation, however, is only one half of the story.
The other half is that if B is to understand the message
'Your father is ill', B must have some knowledge of English. A monoglot speaker of Japanese will not understand
it. If A and B are to communicate verbally in this way they
must share a common public system of communication.
These systems are commonly called 'languages' and have
names such as 'English', 'Japanese', 'Swahili', and so on.
They function as codes. Any two people who know a giv-
en code can transfer messages to one another, because the
code determines the meanings of the signs. If you don't
know the code, you can neither send or receive messages
in it.

Telementation and codes are mutually complementary.
Telementation explains what codes are for, while codes
explain what makes telementation possible. The conjunc-
tion of these two beliefs about communication I shall call
for short 'the language myth'. I call it a myth – the term is
deliberately provocative – because although many people
believe this is actually how verbal communication works,
I think there are good reasons for saying that their belief is
fundamentally mistaken.

What I think actually happens is something much more
complicated, and I shall describe it in detail in Chapter
Nineteen. For the moment, however, the point I wish to
make is that something like the language myth has its roots
in vulgar mindspeak, and they have a long history. This
history goes back at least as far as the philosophers of ancient Greece, most of whom subscribed to the language
myth, although to different versions of it. Now in order to
put both Descartes' view of the mind and Watson's view of
the mind in their proper contexts, you need to realize that
both of them are trying to solve an ancient conundrum that

is raised by the language myth itself.

It is the language myth that sets the agenda both for Descartes and for Watson. Once you see this crucial connexion, it puts the whole debate between Cartesians and anti-Cartesians, between behaviourists and anti-behaviourists, in a new perspective. The conundrum is: where do the ideas come from that are linguistically encoded in English, Japanese and other languages, and which A and B, by selecting the right linguistic signs, can send in messages to each other?

Descartes and Watson propose very different answers, but they are *answers to the same question*. Descartes' answer is that these ideas are put into human heads by God, through the medium of a 'thinking substance' that God, in His wisdom, has made available only to human beings. Watson rejects this answer entirely. His solution is to treat 'ideas' as mistaken projections from language itself. In short, he boldly reverses the traditional priorities of the language myth. Words are not expressions of ideas: the boot is on the other foot. So-called 'ideas' are simply words without the sounds. Hence 'thought' is 'nothing but talking to ourselves'. But in order to talk to yourself you must already have a language to talk in. So language must already be in place before there is any question of thinking. Vulgar mindspeak, according to behaviourists, conceals this fact from us. It misrepresents words as expressions of ideas, rather than explaining *idea* as just another term for words when their linguistic form remains unspecified.

What behaviourism leaves us with is just the language myth in a revised configuration. Messages are still passed from A to B by means of a code. But what are transmitted are just words, not thoughts. What lies behind a word is not a thought, but a potential for stimulating human behaviour.

It is the language myth that likewise furnishes Searle's Chinese room. The assumption is that 'knowing Chinese' is a matter of knowing how to encode and decode messages in Chinese characters. The argument illustrates that just matching one array of characters with another *in accordance with* a code can be done without any understanding of the ideas encoded. But that was already a foregone conclusion, given the premise that Chinese is a code. Searle assumes that there is such a code, but that it is known only to people outside the room. It is rather like arguing that I can wire up a connexion correctly just by following instructions from an electrician, without myself understanding anything about the electrical system. To be sure, I can. But who would have supposed otherwise? The proviso is that I have to understand the instructions. Likewise in the Chinese room, the 'rules' for matching the symbols have to be understood by the operator, even if the symbols themselves are not.

Suppose that we dispense with the person inside the Chinese room, and try postulating that the task of matching input symbols with output symbols is performed by an automatic sorting device which scans the English rules and applies them. Now, it seems, there is a machine 'understanding' the English rules, or doing what amounts to the same thing. To be sure, Searle could recycle the Chinese room argument to show that the English rules could be mechanically applied by an operator who knew no English. And this could go on *ad infinitum* for every successive set of rules in whatever language. But all that would show is a certain desperation to cling to the language myth at all costs.

Until fairly recently, neuroscience and biology had swallowed the 'code' metaphor hook, line and sinker. Not only were *languages* themselves codes, and these codes in turn encoded in codes in the brain, but all 'information' of whatever kind was said to be encoded, or 'represented' in codes, from DNA on. Very occasionally one heard a voice from the scientific community questioning this universal assumption. 'It may be wrong to think that the information in the brain is stored in any "compiled" or "coded" or "propositional" form' (Young 1986: 50). But this was very much the exception that proved the rule.

A challenge to the whole notion of codes and rules arrived in the form of 'connectionism'. The basic connectionist idea is that within a neural network the strength of the connections between nodes varies over time as a result of how frequently these connections are used. Heavier 'traffic' will reinforce a connection and lighter 'traffic' weaken it. This will affect the behaviour of the network as a whole and its capacity for dealing with 'messages'.

Exactly how this model can be deployed to throw light on the workings of the mind is still a matter of controversy. No one knows how many neural networks there are in the brain, or how these networks themselves interconnect. A cautious conclusion is that the operation of networks might explain 'at least certain aspects of the mind' at 'one level up from single nerve cells' (Rose 2006: 188). But even that vague promissory note would be regarded by many as over-optimistic.

Chapter Eight: The silent mind

The language myth gives rise to a very narrow view of what thinking is, or at least the kind of thinking that eventually issues in speech or writing. Once a telementational view of communication is in place, it seems attractive to suppose that thinking itself – or a certain form of thinking – is nothing other than a kind of inner speech. I have already mentioned the behaviourist version of this theory. But it goes back at least as far as the time of Plato. In *Theaetetus*, Socrates puts it very lucidly:

> It seems to me that the soul when it thinks is simply carrying on a discussion in which it asks itself questions and answers them itself, affirms and denies. And when it arrives at something definite, either by a gradual process or a sudden leap, when it affirms one thing consistently and without divided counsel, we call this its judgment. So, in my view, to judge is to make a statement which is not addressed to another person or spoken aloud, but silently addressed to oneself. (*Theaetetus* 190a)

This is, as it were, telementation turned back upon itself, or mindspeak coming to its own rescue. Similar remarks are to be found elsewhere in Plato's dialogues (e.g. *Sophist* 263e, where the identity of thought with unvoiced verbalization is taken for granted as uncontroversial). That, according to Socrates, is exactly right. This is not just a vague claim to the effect that thinking is 'rather like' talking: thought *is* speech, but with the sound turned off. It supplies an explanation of what rational thinking consists in; namely, an internal dialogue having the same kind of structure as conversation. If we understand what it is to converse with someone, then we need not be puzzled by what thinking is. Furthermore, although Socrates introduces it for the particular purpose of explaining judgment, the same idea can easily be extended to other types of mental act or mental state. (For example, uncertainty can be construed as the outcome of a dialogue in which no firm conclusion is reached; optimism as the outcome of a dialogue in which promises are made and their fulfilment confidently anticipated; fear as the outcome of a dialogue in which threats are made, and so on.) By this means, one of the great mysteries about the mind seems to be dispelled, i.e. the mystery surrounding the nature of mental processes. They are not just *analogues* of those encountered overtly in speech, but the same processes not carried as far as overt manifestation.

This Socratic account of thinking left its mark on many later discussions of the mind. One among many is to be found in Thomas Hobbes' *Leviathan*. For Hobbes, there is no room for doubt about the relation between thought and speech.

> The generall use of Speech, is to transferre our Mentall Discourse, into Verbal; or the Trayne of our Thoughts, into a Trayne of Words. (Hobbes 1651: I, iv)

For Hobbes, the 'Trayne of Thoughts' determines the 'Trayne of Words':

> By *Consequence*, or TRAYNE of Thoughts, I understand that succession of one Thought to another, which is called (to distinguish it from Discourse in words) *Mentall Discourse*.

When a man thinketh on any thing whatsoever, His next
Thought after, is not altogether so casuall as it seems to
be. Not every Thought to every Thought succeeds indif-
ferently. (Hobbes 1651: I.iii)

Hobbes clearly envisages a close correspondence between the two 'Traynes': exactly how close is never made
clear. But the reader is left to assume that the linear sequence of words does in general reflect the sequence of
thoughts expressed. There is no reason to think otherwise
if the thoughts in question are the product of a silent internal process with a temporal structure that anticipates
speech.

This belief is still going strong in modern psychology.
We find erudite academic papers discussing 'the speaker's
linearization problem', which starts from the assumption
that speaking involves 'a mapping of thoughts (intentions,
feelings, etc.) onto language' (Levelt 1981: 305). Now this
alleged mapping 'problem' would make no sense at all
unless it were assumed that somewhere the speaker has
available an internal store of words (or their silent ghostly
prototypes) waiting to be assembled in the right order, i.e.
to match the thought sequence already laid down in 'inner
speech'.

A parallel development to that which produces 'inner
speech' as the explanation of thought appears elsewhere
than in the Western tradition. In India in the fifth century,
we find Bhartrhari maintaining that the act of thinking just
is verbalization at some preliminary level. (For interpreta-
tions of Bhartrhari's thesis, as well as criticisms of it by
Buddhist scholars, see Matilal 1990: 133-41.)

It is worth noting that both Plato and Bhartrhari were
highly articulate members of a literate society. They could
read and write. They were entirely familiar with the notion
that a word and its overt form or forms are not indissolu-
bly linked, i.e. that sounds and written characters can be
equally valid ways of producing *the same word*. Grasping
this equivalence is crucial to the concept of 'thinking' that

Socrates advances. I suggest that if the Athens of the age of Socrates had been a pre-literate community (as it had been a few centuries earlier), the view of thinking proposed in *Theaetetus* would never have occurred to him. And if it had occurred to him, it would have seemed ridiculous. The point is unprovable, but it merits consideration. The advent of writing as an independent mode of communication seems to me to have implications not only for the way people view 'thought' but for the way they view 'speech' as well. Once speech and writing are seen as alternatives, there is a strong inclination to regard thinking as an independent process involved in both.

The elaboration of the language myth in the Western tradition is a by-product of the fact that literate societies live in a different world from pre-literate societies. The two worlds have a different understanding of time. If you do not have writing available, you cannot leave laws or instructions for your descendants. You have to rely on persuading your contemporaries to do things after your death. But that is to rely on their memories and their sense of obligation. The written document is the first (imperfect) approximation to 'timeless' communication that human ingenuity has devised. We are still living with its imperfections.

The reason why the Socratic explanation of thinking as inner speech will not do as it stands is that it is vacuous in the same way as the notorious 'homunculus fallacy', ridiculed by generations of schoolchildren. (According to this, A's hunger is explained as due to the fact that there is a little man inside A who is hungry. This 'explanation' does nothing more than defer the problem, given that nothing has been said about why the little man inside A is hungry. Is there another little man inside the first little man?) The case of inner speech is not quite like this, but sufficiently similar to be ineffectual in the same way. For the words of inner speech presumably have meanings, like the words of audible speech. However, if the meanings of audible words are the ideas those words convey (as the language myth assures us), then it would seem that the same ideas have to do double duty as the meanings of inaudible words too. In that case, we are no nearer to an explanation of what thinking is. Conveying ideas was supposedly what distinguished audible speech from gibberish, and inner speech was invoked with the sole aim of explaining what thinking is. It fails to do so if it turns out to be no more than a silent echo of what goes on in audible speech all the time. For *that* was exactly what we wanted to find out in the first place. It is rather like explaining a drawing as a picture of an image in the artist's imagination, and then describing the image as being just like the drawing, but without any visible marks on the paper.

It is sometimes claimed that the homunculus fallacy can be avoided by 'homuncular functionalism' (Rose 2006: 85-121). The idea is that one can 'solve the man-in-the-head problem by breaking it down into manageable chunks' (Rose 2006: 120); that is, into separate functional modules in the brain. But it is hard to see how replacing one homunculus by a whole family of homunculi solves anything. It simply gives rise to the further problem of explaining how 'those little homunculi cooperate with one another appropriately' (Rose 2006: 87). In effect, we are back with the puzzle mentioned at the end of Chapter Two: the clock lacks any individual component for keeping time.

Chapter Nine: The linguistic mind

Can you imagine a science-fiction race of intelligent beings on Mars who have minds but no language? Yes, it's fairly easy. Can you imagine another race who have language but no minds? That is harder, and the difficulty says something about the way people tend to view the connexion between language and mind. There seems to be no point in creatures being capable of producing the works of Aristotle and the plays of Shakespeare if they have no thoughts to express.

This is still the basic assumption in modern linguistics. It may come as a shock to those who suppose that modern linguistics is a rigorous 'science' and has long parted company with the antiquated ideas about language that underlay both traditional prescriptive grammar and old-fashioned text-based 'philology' to realize that the language myth underlies all three. One of the classic examples of the language myth as presented in its modern form by a major linguistic theorist is the influential account of the 'speech circuit' given in Ferdinand de Saussure's *Cours de linguistique générale*. This describes two imaginary individuals, *A* and *B*, engaged in conversation.

> Suppose that the opening of the circuit is in *A*'s brain, where mental facts (concepts) are associated with representations of the linguistic sounds (sound-images) that are used for their expression. A given concept unlocks a

corresponding sound-image in the brain; this purely *psychological* phenomenon is followed in turn by a *physiological* process: the brain transmits an impulse corresponding to the image to the organs used in producing sounds. Then sound waves travel from the mouth of *A* to the ear of *B*: a purely *physical* process. Next, the circuit continues in *B*, but the order is reversed: from the ear to the brain, the physiological transmission of the sound-image; in the brain, the psychological association of the image with the corresponding concept. If *B* then speaks, the new act will follow – from his brain to *A*'s – exactly the same course as the first act and pass through the same successive phases. (Saussure 1922: 11-12)

Here we have exactly the kind of telementation-plus-code model that the language myth embodies. There are a sender and a receiver in whose brains are stored a repository of ideas (*concepts*) associated with sound-images (*images acoustiques*). The sole function of speech is evidently to ensure that *B* receives an idea corresponding to that which prompted *A*'s utterance. It is interesting to note that it goes unstated that *A* and *B* are speakers of the same language, i.e. users of the same code: this is taken for granted. For if the model is to explain communication, *B* has to be familiar with the sounds and sound-images in which A encodes the message, as well as being familiar with the concepts that *A* is thus expressing.

Some psychologists now repeat the Saussurean model of speech communication as if it summarized uncontroversial, well-established facts. According to one, the linguistic sign functions effectively because

> a speaker and a hearer can call on identical entries in their mental dictionaries. The speaker has a thought, makes a sound, and counts on the listener to hear the sound and recover that thought. (Pinker 1999: 3)

This, apart from conflating facts with hypotheses,

makes no bones about supposing that the 'mental diction-aries' of *A* and *B* have to contain 'identical' entries. If they are different, whatever *B* 'recovers' from the sound will not be what *A* wanted to say.

No behaviourist could accept the Saussurean model for obvious reasons. The first is because of the important role it assigns to unobservables. Since *A*'s concepts are as un-observable as *B*'s, there is no way to tell whether they cor-respond exactly or not. The same applies to the postulated 'sound-images'. The only elements of the circuit that can be examined objectively in any 'scientific' way (i.e. meas-ured and analysed instrumentally) are the sound waves and the movements of the vocal organs that produce them. But Saussure quite happily introduced unobservables into his linguistic theorizing because, unlike Bloomfield, he was not a behaviourist. Furthermore, far from basing his linguistic theorizing on phonetics, Saussure went to the opposite extreme and denied that the study of phonetics was properly part of linguistics. For Saussure, the key to the study of linguistics is the linguistic sign, and the lin-guistic sign is present in both speaker and hearer only as a mental unit, i.e. an internal psychological association be-tween sound-image and concept. How it got there in the first place is not the linguist's concern.

The second reason why a behaviourist would be un-happy with Saussure's account is that no mention is made of any actions that ensue from or accompany speech. For instance, *A* does not point or gesture while speaking, nor does *B*, for instance, get up and close the window. The speech circuit seems to be symmetrical and self-contained. *B* makes a vocal response to *A*'s vocal utterance; or if there is any non-vocal response, Saussure tells us nothing about it. It lies outside the concerns of the linguist. This again is in keeping with the language myth, which says nothing about what happens when thoughts have been successfully transmitted. There is no explanatory attempt to integrate language with non-linguistic activities. It is as if the send-ing and receiving of linguistic signs were itself the sole purpose of language.

Saussure's model can be elaborated in greater detail than Saussure ever bothered to do. One such elaboration (Moulton 1970) distinguishes eleven 'successive stages' in the transmission of a message from A to B: (1) semantic encoding, (2) grammatical encoding, (3) phonological encoding, (4) from brain to speech organs, (5) movements of the speech organs, (6) vibrations of the air molecules, (7) vibrations of the ear, (8) from ear to brain, (9) phonological decoding, (10) grammatical decoding, (11) semantic decoding. But the model is still recognizably a telementational model derived from the language myth. The basic assumption is 'that A has some sort of "idea" or "thought" or "meaning" that he wants to communicate to B' (Moulton 1970: 24). This assumption dictates the form of the 'task' that A must tackle. 'The task that now faces A is: How can he get this idea into such a shape that it can be communicated in the language he is using?' (Moulton 1970: 24).

This task is initially a mental task, and stages (1), (2) and (3) must belong to what Saussure calls the 'psychological' section of the circuit, although Saussure does not recognize these 'encoding' procedures, because in his version the initial concepts seem to come with the appropriate sound-images already attached. Nor, for an exactly parallel reason, does Saussure recognize the corresponding 'decoding' tasks that B has. But Saussure's model is a code model for all that: it ultimately requires a matching between what A sends and what B receives.

We sometimes hear of three separate codes involved, all interconnected:

> During speech transmission, the speaker's linguistic code of words and sentences is transformed into physiological and physical codes – in other words, into corresponding sets of muscle movements and air vibrations – before being reconverted into a linguistic code at the listener's end. (Denes and Pinson 1963: 8)

But this is hopelessly confused. It makes no more sense to speak of the correlation between (1) muscle movements and (2) air vibration as being code-based than it would to describe the connexion between (1) going out in the rain and (2) getting wet as governed by a code. You don't get wet by knowing a code, or because Nature has put a code of her own in place. Scientists who speak of the 'genetic code' in DNA, or 'coding operations' taking place continuously in the nervous system (Pribram 1971: 66-82), are at best mixing their metaphors, and at worst talking gobbledegook. Codes are human conventions. What might be true in the case of speech is something rather different: that natural correlations between muscle movements and air vibrations might themselves be made the basis of a linguistic code. But I doubt that too, for reasons I shall go on to explain in the following chapter.

Chapter Ten: The mind demythologized

A first step towards demythologizing discussions of the mind is to reject the language myth and all the 'mentalist' trappings that go with it. There are various reasons for this.

1. Thought-transference.

The first is that the whole telementation component of the language myth is unproven and unprovable. We cannot know whether our ideas are the same as other people's because of a simple difficulty stated long ago with exemplary clarity by one of the great philosophers of language, John Locke. It is all the more telling because Locke himself was committed to his own version of the language myth: in his *Essay Concerning Human Understanding* he was trying to support it, not dismiss it. Nevertheless, he conceded that

> every man has so inviolable a liberty to make words stand for what idea he pleases, that no one hath the power to make others have the same ideas in their minds that he has, when they use the same words that he does. (Locke 1706: III.ii.8)

It would be illusory to suppose that there is any test that *A* can apply to make certain that *B* has grasped exactly what *A* means by the words *A* utters. Supplying definitions is no guarantee, since exactly the same problem will arise with regard to the words comprising the definition. That solution simply embarks on a definitional regress. Dictionaries are full of circularities and dead ends, as the more intelligent lexicographers are fully aware. The circularities arise when a chain of definitions ultimately leads inquirers back to the word they started with; and dead ends when inquirers are led to terms for which the dictionary has no entry at all. What this points to is the futility of trying to specify the idea associated with a word by substituting other words. Substitution may well be helpful up to a certain point and for certain purposes, but it falls short of giving a certain identification of any of the ideas expressed.

In everyday conversation this definitional impasse may not matter very much, partly because the triviality of the subject matter does not call for exact definitions, and partly because verbal communication can usually be supplemented by non-verbal communication if the need arises. But it is nevertheless an illusion to suppose that behind the words we use every day lies a hidden domain of clearly delineated ideas, to which we can gain access by probing the words themselves.

There is an even more compelling reason why I think Locke was right about this, although Locke himself does not mention it. In order to ascertain whether you understand exactly what I am saying, I would first have to be sure what that is. But on reflection it often seems difficult to determine, even in very simple cases. For example, I unhesitatingly use the word *daffodil* when talking about certain flowers that appear in my garden every spring. But what is my idea of a 'daffodil'? It must cover more than just the particular flowers in my garden. But how much more? My knowledge of and interest in botany are not sufficient for me to say exactly what I mean when I use the word. Perhaps, if I am honest, all I mean is: 'flower of a species bearing a superficial resemblance to those I see every spring in my garden'. But in that case, no one could know what my idea of a daffodil was unless they were acquainted with my garden: and in any case that idea is certainly not going to be conveyed to them simply by my uttering the word *daffodil*. Similarly, when others use the word *daffodil* I hope they are talking about the same kind of flowers as I am; I may *hope* so, but I cannot be sure.

Some people might say: 'There is nothing wrong with that. It's just that you have only a vague idea of what a daffodil is. But so have many other people. That does not prevent the word *daffodil* from being perfectly adequate for most communicational purposes.' However, once this is admitted and brought out into the open, it torpedoes the telementational component of the language myth. For what it amounts to saying is that we all use words on the limited basis of our own experience (e.g. the interest I may or may not take in the flowers in my garden that I call 'daffodils'). But it would be silly for each of us to suppose that our personal experience is somehow mentally transmissible to others as a basis for understanding what we say, let alone that this transmission can be magically effected by the simple expedient of uttering a word.

2. Codes.

I do not believe in telementation and I do not believe in codes either; at least not in the kind of code required by the language myth. The job that codes are asked to do, as far as the language myth is concerned, is supply a *public* basis for communication, such that *the same words* mean *the same thing* for all members of the linguistic community. Words have to be, in brief, *invariants*: invariant as between one user and another, and invariant across different occasions of use.

Now I do not believe that English, or French, or any other language, are codes in this sense. I know this from my own experience of trying to communicate with others. I know, for example, that other people who speak English often use such words as *soon, next, quickly, difficult, just, honest, democratic, tolerant* – I could extend this list for

pages on end – in ways that seem to me in the circumstances odd, quite unjustified, or even outrageous. So if
there is any code regulating the way these speakers use
these words, where is it? It will not do to say that we each
have our own mental code for using English. That, indeed,
is an admission that the public code is a myth.

I cannot see how the members of a linguistic community as vast as all those who regard themselves as speakers
of English could possibly have been able to learn such a
code in the first place. English is not like a system of traffic
lights, where the number of signals can be counted on the
fingers of one hand, and those who are in doubt about what
the signals mean can consult the *Highway Code*. English,
by any count, has *millions* of words. How could we *all*
have learnt what *all* of them mean? The answer is that we
couldn't, and didn't. English is not a code but a congeries
of conflicting usages – a fact which grammarians try to
ignore by approving some usages, which by oversimpli-
fication they reduce to 'rules', and condemning others as
'incorrect' (i.e. infringements of their 'rules'). But none of
these attempts to force the diversity of 'English' into the
Procrustean bed of codes stands up to a moment's serious
scrutiny in practice. If there are any such linguistic codes,
they must be more honoured in the breach than the observ-
ance.

3. Language and the world.

A third reason why I think the language myth has to
be rejected is that it misrepresents my experience of communication. As far as I can see, people engage in communication with others mainly in order to connect with the
world and influence, if possible, what goes on in it. But the
language myth *excludes* the world. The world is allowed
in only at one remove in the guise of *mental* units or events
('ideas'). Daffodils do not belong to any language, only
the concept 'daffodil', and then only with the proviso that
a language has a word 'expressing' that concept.

Among theories of the mind that rely most heavily on the language myth is the currently popular HOT (Higher Order Thought) theory (Rosenthal 2005). According to this, what is characteristic of human consciousness is not just having thoughts but having meta-thoughts, i.e. thoughts about thoughts. This is typically manifested in being able to *report* one's thoughts. When we speak, according to HOT theorists, 'we put words to our mental states, and convey those thoughts to others' (Rosenthal 2005: 72). This is telementation of the crudest stamp. Without it, Rosenthal's account of the mind cannot even get started.

If the language myth and the models it sponsors are rejected, does this mean that all talk about the mind is banned? I do not think so. Is there a better way of thinking about human communication which does not lead us into the same traps? I think there is, and I shall come to it shortly. But first I wish to comment on some more sophisticated confusions about the mind that are the legacy of the language myth.

Chapter Eleven: The mind located

Do you think (as most linguists seem to nowadays) that in order to read a book such as this you need the internal equivalent of a good English dictionary, plus an internal grammar to go with it? If so, it seems natural to ask: where, then, is this linguistic equipment to be found?

One's vulgar mind is vulgarly supposed to be located in one's head. (It is rare to hear anyone declare that they believe their mind is situated in their elbow or their left knee, and I can think offhand of no work of fiction in which such a bizarre location is postulated.) There is indeed a certain overlap between vulgar mindspeak and vulgar brainspeak. Someone outstandingly clever is commonly said to be 'brainy'. A brilliant idea is a 'brain-wave'. The originator of a successful plan is 'the brain behind it'. To have an obsession about something is to have it 'on the brain'. A conundrum is a 'brain-teaser'. So there seems undoubtedly to be some popular presumption of a connexion between mind and brain, even if it is not very clear exactly what this connexion is.

A range of possibilities is available. At one end there are those who believe that a search for the location of the mind is a misguided enterprise from the start, because the mind does not exist. 'There is no more an entity called the mind, from which what we describe as mental phenomena proceed, than there is an entity called digestion presiding over the digestive processes' (Kenyon 1941: 2).

'For the neurologist, there is no such thing as the mind' (Nathan 1987: 514). To the 'ain't-no-such-thing' school belong those known as 'eliminative materialists'. As Max Velmans points out, their problem is that doubting the existence of consciousness is self-defeating, because 'unless one has consciousness one cannot have doubts' (Velmans 2000: 32).

Eliminativists sometimes attempt to wriggle out of this kind of criticism by alleging that it begs the question against them. According to one leading eliminativist, Paul Churchland, the argument takes the following form: the statement that mental states do not exist expresses a belief, which ought not to exist if the statement is true. So the assumption that eliminative materialism is true allegedly entails that it cannot be true, which is self-contradictory. All this shows, however, Churchland claims, is that the meaningfulness of the eliminativist claim 'must have some different source' than the expression of that belief (Churchland 1988: 48). Here Churchland in turn begs the question in his own favour: i.e. by assuming that the objector is committed to a psychocentric theory of meaning. But Velmans' objection stands. Whatever theory of semantics you hold, the claim 'I have no beliefs' is still self-stultifying; just as the claim 'Every proposition is false' is self-stultifying, regardless of what theory of truth you hold.

Others allow the existence of the mind, but claim that it is not an inner 'repository which is permitted to house objects that something called "the physical world" is forbidden to house' (Ryle 1949: 190). Then there is the view that the mind does indeed exist, but turns out to be identical with the brain, or some part of the brain. It has even been suggested (Palma 2004: 614) that the words *mind* and *brain* can be regarded as mere spelling variants. But that suggestion seems more likely to indicate ignorance of English orthography than deep insight into the mechanisms of the cerebral cortex.

The whole sorry muddle stems from the view of 'ideas' sponsored by the language myth. It is supposed that if ideas exist as individual entities, they must exist *somewhere*, and if they exist in association with words, *somewhere* is presumably wherever the words are. But why stop there? The muddle ramifies at an alarming rate. Ideas can apparently exist not only in the mind, but in books, drawings and buildings. Any vehicle of expression can harbour an idea. There is no shortage of accommodation.

One conclusion of this line of reasoning is that wherever the ideas are, the mind must be too. The germ of this can be seen in Ryle's observation that 'Overt intelligent performances are not clues to the workings of minds; they are those workings' (Ryle 1949: 57). But nowadays it has been taken much further by philosophers who talk overtly of *distributed mind* and *distributed cognition* (which Ryle did not). This is certainly a new brand of mindspeak. The implication seems to be that we should not regard the mind just as something in the head, or as goings-on in the brain, but as something, or as goings-on, in the body and the local environment too.

The irony is that this conclusion seems to have been reached in the following way. Those who saw (rightly) that there was something amiss in sealing the mind hermetically inside the head leapt to the erroneous conclusion that it might be somewhere *else*, i.e. outside the cranium. They failed to see that the concept of *location* itself was the root of the problem. You do not solve it by dividing the mind generously between all available locations.

Is this currently fashionable talk of distributed mind merely metaphorical? Those who adopt it do not seem anxious to acknowledge its metaphorical status. Some indeed are willing to claim, for instance, that 'in certain circumstances' certain 'artefacts and other external structures are literally cognitive', and that 'in certain circumstances, along with the brain and body interacting with them, they *are* the mind' (Sutton 2004: 506. Italics in the original.). But anyone brought up on vulgar mindspeak will feel no inclination whatever to say that your pocket calculator is part of your mind (but part of your mind that you happen to keep in your pocket). Nor is there any obvious advantage in adopting this way of speaking. On the contrary, it appears to open the door to all kinds of confusions.

Why? Because using a pocket calculator is no more an extended form of thinking than riding a bicycle is an extended form of walking. It is a different kind of activity altogether. Using a pocket calculator effectively to obtain one's ends doubtless requires intelligence; but so does riding a bicycle. Nor does anyone doubt that the calculator was the product of design by intelligent human beings. So was the bicycle. None of this licenses the bizarre conclusion that either of these machines has a mind or is part of a mind.

Is it looking for the mind to be *somewhere* (whether inside or outside the head) that is the fundamental mistake? Can it be avoided by agreeing with A.J. Ayer that 'the mind has no position in space – it is by definition not the sort of thing that can have a position in space' (Ayer 1950: 73-4)? I do not think so, because that risks compounding the muddle. There just is no question of what the mind 'is by definition'. One can, of course, decide to define the word *mind* in such a way that what it designates has no position in space: it is easy enough to do that, but what remains obscure to me is why anyone would choose to adopt that kind of stipulative definition. After all, it makes perfectly good sense to say that Albert had a brilliant idea while walking on Brighton pier, and not very much sense to add that of course his mind wasn't on Brighton pier, nor the brilliant idea either. That sounds too much like saying: 'I didn't realize how late it was until I got home, but of course it would be absurd to suppose that's where the realization occurred.'

The fuss about the location of the mind (including whether it has a location at all) is symptomatic of a failure to grasp something important – the role of vulgar mindspeak in our understanding of experience. The mistake of those who insist on a location for the mind is on a par with supposing that it ought to be possible to find the exact place on (or off) the football pitch where the match was won. The mistake of those who deny that the mind has any location is on a par with supposing that winning the match had nothing to do with what happened on the pitch at all.

Chapter Twelve: The self-evident mind

There is a great temptation to suppose that merely being able to ask the question 'Do I have a mind?' points unmistakably in favour of the answer 'Yes'. How else could I formulate the question? This is mindspeak tugging at its own shoelaces.

Being able to ask 'Do I have a million pounds?' or 'Do I have a fairy godmother?' does not usually convince us that we *do* have a million pounds or a fairy godmother. So why should being able to ask 'Do I have a mind?' be any more persuasive? The answer is that what makes it *appear* persuasive is our tacit acceptance of certain assumptions about language. If we believe the traditional language myth, then it follows as the night follows day that anyone who speaks English must have a mind.

It is remarkable how many philosophers have been taken in by this. Here is one version of the argument, as presented by Daniel Dennett in his book *Kinds of Minds*:

> It is beyond serious dispute [ ] that you and I each have a mind. How do I know you have a mind? Because anybody who can understand my words is automatically addressed by my pronoun "you," and only things with minds can understand. There are computer-driven devices that can read books for the blind: they convert a page of visible text into a stream of audible words, but they don't understand the words they read and hence are not

addressed by any "you" they encounter; it passes right
through them and addresses whoever listens to – and
understands – the stream of spoken words. That's how I
know that you, gentle reader/listener, have a mind. So do
I. Take my word for it. (Dennett 1996: 8)

Taking Dennett's word for it is not – I imagine – what
grammarians are likely to do, since he is so obviously confused about how English pronouns work. It simply isn't
true that the pronoun you in a written text addresses anyone who happens to read it. But suppose we overlook
that rather obvious howler, the rest is no more convincing. Skipping the bit about pronouns, Dennett's contention
boils down to this: anyone who can read or write such a
paragraph must have a mind.

What is wrong with that can be seen by comparing it
with: 'Any creature capable of walking up these stairs must
have a podome'. The claim is vacuous unless we are told
what the word *podome* means. Otherwise, we learn nothing except that a podome is something allegedly essential
for creatures who can walk up stairs. We are not told why
it is essential, or even that having a podome is *what makes
it possible to walk up stairs*.

Curiously, Dennett makes his own claim to have a mind
depend on his understanding his own words and those of
others. But nothing in the paragraph quoted above dem-
onstrates to the reader that Dennett understands his own
claim. You may understand what Dennett has written, or
think you do, but that can hardly be construed as serious
evidence that Dennett himself understands it. The reader is
given no explanation of what a mind is and none of what
'understanding' is supposed to consist in. So what is going
on here? Dennett, it becomes obvious, is tacitly relying
on the assumption that he and you are fluent in, and will
recognize that you are both fluent in, 'the same language',
and that this language already includes the word *mind*.
Without that assumption, his reasoning collapses.

Dennett's argument is also a bad argument for another

reason. The rhetorical trick by which your possession of a mind is made to appear a rational conclusion following from your possession of certain linguistic abilities hinges on smuggling in a stipulative definition of *mind*. If spelled out in full it would read roughly as follows: 'By *mind* I (Dennett) mean – at least for purposes of this dodgy argument – whatever mechanisms or capacities are required for the possession of language'. Thus in the end Dennett's argument that supposedly puts the matter 'beyond serious dispute' boils down to no more than Dennett's determination to use the word *mind* in this way. It is a prime example of how to convince yourself that you have a mind by refusing to use the word *mind* without that assumption.

On this basis, Dennett proceeds to construct a bogus dilemma:

> Obviously, we can know to a moral certainty (which is all that matters) that some things have minds and other things don't.
>
> But we don't yet know *how* we know these facts; the strength of our intuitions about such cases is no guarantee of their reliability. (Dennett 1996: 15)

What is being slipped in here under the guise of 'moral certainty' is the assumption that it's OK to tread on an ant or a worm, because we 'know' they don't have minds (whereas it would be culpable to extinguish life wantonly in a creature that *does* have a mind). But although we already 'know' this about ants and worms, we don't know *how* we know it. And this is where philosophical assistance (from Dennett) is required.

If you have read Dennett's book thus far, you can guess what the answer is going to be, because Dennett has already built it into his opening argument. Mindless creatures are those who cannot communicate to other members of their species by means of language or something very like it.

It is consequently curious that Dennett has nothing to

say about the great amount of work that has been done in recent years on teaching systems of symbolic communication to other primates, and the great amount of controversy that has surrounded that research. It seems now to be fairly well established experimentally that it is possible to teach a bonobo to understand 'spoken English utterances of a grammatical and semantic complexity equal to (and in some cases surpassing) that mastered by a normal two-and-a-half-year-old human child' (Savage-Rumbaugh, Shanker and Taylor 1998: v). This fact, according to one of the leading researchers in the field, shows us 'that we are not alone among God's creatures to have been blessed with the gift of mind' (Savage-Rumbaugh, Shanker and Taylor 1998: 7). Presumably Dennett would have to agree. But those who reject the claim question whether the abilities monkeys have shown in dealing with verbal and other symbols is genuinely 'linguistic'.

The result is that a debate about the word *mind* is transformed into a debate about the word *language*: the question 'What is a mind?' is replaced by 'What is language?'. I confess to being unable to muster up much enthusiasm for this new form of debate. It was a mistake to treat language as a criterion for having a mind in the first place.

Dennett's argument ultimately boils down to this: 'You and I both know, and know that we know, that we understand what we are saying to each other. How could we possibly make sense of that unless we had minds?' A slightly less question-begging version of the same argument is the following:

> We routinely ascribe states with content to persons, animals, and even some nonbiological systems. If we had no such practice – if we were to stop attributing to our fellow human beings beliefs, desires, emotions, and the like – our communal life would surely suffer a massive collapse. [...] Moreover, it is by attributing these states to ourselves that we come to understand ourselves as cognizers and agents. (Kim 2006: 240)

But this will not do either. The question is not what life would be like if our language lacked the resources of vulgar mindspeak. The question is whether having those resources in itself makes the existence of the mind self-evident. It does not. To see that this is so, imagine a society of devoutly religious Martians, in whose language everything that happens is explicitly attributed to divine intervention. Thus their terms for belief, desire, emotion, etc. mean, when translated into English, 'what the gods caused you to think', 'what the gods caused you to want', 'what the gods caused you to feel', etc. It will be perfectly true that deploying this Martian vocabulary is absolutely central to life on Mars and the sense Martians make of it. But this centrality does not somehow guarantee of itself that the assumption of ubiquitous divine intervention is correct, or that the existence of the gods is thereby assured.

Chapter Thirteen: The verbalized mind

Another way philosophers have dodged problems about the existence of the mind is by just assuming that knowing how to use a word is the same as having a concept.

In Peter Geach's book *Mental Acts*, we are told that it is a sufficient condition for anyone's having the concept of *so-and-so* 'that he should have mastered the intelligent use (including the use in made-up sentences) of a word for *so-and-so* in some language':

> Thus: if somebody knows how to use the English word "red", he has a concept of red; if he knows how to use the first-person pronoun, he has a concept of *self*; if he knows how to use the negative construction in some language, he has a concept of negation. (Geach 1957: 12-13)

The reason why this will not do as it stands is that without reliance on tacit support from the language myth it is not even coherent. Might not people with different colour vision, but all speaking English, call somewhat different things 'red'? And if so, mustn't there be not just 'a concept of red' but many concepts of red? Similarly, the notion of 'knowing how to use the first-person pronoun' and 'knowing how to use the negative construction' both rely implicitly not only on a code model of languages but on the assumption that the grammars of different languages are just variants of an underlying common code. If this is not the assumption, then one would have to be careful to distinguish between, say, the English concept of 'self' and the Latin concept of 'self', or the English concept of 'negation' and the French concept of 'negation'. Once the identification of concepts is tied to grammatical peculiarities and usages that vary from one linguistic community to the next, the advantage of appealing to mastery of words in order to explicate concepts turns into a liability. For it is now quite unclear what justification there is for classifying these various concepts by applying the same general labels (e.g. 'self' and 'negation').

What is happening here is that Geach is trying to resurrect the ancient language-myth assumption that the meaning of a word is an idea, but he has tried to avoid the term *meaning* in favour of *use*. What this fails to recognize is just how slippery a concept 'use' is, and Geach slides about with it in all directions. Perhaps I know how to use a word sufficiently well for some purposes, but not for others: for instance, I might know how to use the expression *bird flu* sufficiently well for the purposes of talking about the threat of an epidemic with my next-door neighbour, but not nearly well enough to sustain a serious discussion with a virologist. Charitably, the virologist might say of me: 'He has a vague idea of what bird flu is, but also various misconceptions.' But if misconceptions and potential misconceptions also count as concepts, it seems there must be an endless variety of 'bird flu' concepts, depending on degrees of ignorance. And if that is so, it seems we would do better to stop talking about 'knowing the/a way of using the expression *bird flu*' and start analysing the degrees of ignorance. For there is no *one* concept of 'bird flu' associated with that expression.

In many cases it will be difficult, and rather arbitrary, to decide how many concepts correspond to each linguistic item. If I am said to have mastered the use, say, of 'the English preposition *of*', does that give me just one concept? Or as many as there are distinguishable uses of that preposition? Geach simply pre-empts any such inquiry by declaring that 'it does not even make sense to ask just how many concepts are exercised in a given judgment' (Geach 1957: 15). But in that case, it throws no light on my mental activities at all to talk about what I can do with the word *of* (other than – tautologically – use it when speaking or writing English).

The problem is exacerbated in Geach's case by his insistence that 'concepts', as far as he is concerned, are subjective and personal: a concept is 'a mental capacity belonging to a particular person'. But then he makes matters worse for himself when he tries to identify 'the same concept' both as between different individuals and across different languages:

> The subjective nature of concepts does not however imply that it is improper to speak of two people as "having the same concept"; conformably to my explanation of the term "concept", this will mean that they have the same mental capacity, i.e. can do essentially the same things. Thus, if each of two men has mastered the intelligent use of the negative construction in his own language, we may say that they have the same mental capacity, the same concept; they both have the concept of negation. (Geach 1957: 14)

It is interesting to note here the shift from talking about 'a concept of negation' to talking about 'the concept of negation'. In other words, the language myth is now being supplemented by a latent doctrine of language universals. It sounds as if these bland assumptions about interlingual identities conceal a naive theory of translation that the author is unwilling to articulate explicitly.

Geach finally falls headlong into the linguistic pit he has been busy digging. He considers the question: 'if a Frenchman who knows no English knows the use of the French adjective "rouge", does he know the use of the English adjective "red"?' The casuistic answer Geach supplies is that in one sense of *knowing the use of* he does not (since we all agree he knows no English); but in another sense he does, because – claims Geach – the French and English uses are the same. The ingenuity of this argument is matched only by its absurdity. The test of whether I know the use(s) of the French word *rouge* is whether I know how to use it in conversation with a French person in French. My knowledge of English is an irrelevance.

Words are often said to be the mind's 'tools', or 'tools' for thinking. This idea leads on to treating having a mind as having 'the capacity to acquire the ability to operate with symbols in such a way that it is one's own activity that makes them symbols and confers meaning on them' (Kenny 1973: 47). This canny formulation is of some relevance to the 'Chinese room' argument discussed in Chapter Six. For there what allegedly made the sorting of Chinese symbols meaningless was the fact that they were meaningful only *outside* the room. The activities of the sorter were apparently unimpeded by failure to understand them as words at all.

But this is only one half of the story. The other half is that what the sorter did – the sorter's own activity – made them symbols of a different kind, conferring on them meanings that had nothing to do (except coincidentally) with the Chinese language. The meanings in question were determined by the sorter's matching instructions, and implemented by his execution of those instructions. And that would still have been the case even if the symbols had been just arbitrary geometrical shapes. What the sorter is doing is still a meaningful activity. And if the sorting had been done by machine, the same holds.

The lesson to be learnt from this is that there are other kinds of symbols than words and other kinds of meaning than verbal meaning. Any systematically integrated pattern of activities yields meaning, irrespective of whether words are involved or not. The Chinese room argument depends on tacitly restricting the concept of meaning to the verbal kind.

Those theorists who assign top priority to the mind's

verbal activities often seem to assume that we never have any difficulty in saying what we mean. David Rosenthal claims that

> although others must sometimes tell us how to take their words, we need never do this for ourselves. We know automatically what construction to place on our own words. The best explanation of this knowledge is [...] that we come to be aware of what we say by being aware of what mental state our words express. (Rosenthal 2005: 97)

Here again we have the language myth brought in like a *deus ex machina* to supply a quite naive 'explanation' of how the mind works. It is not just an implausible explanation: it is not an explanation at all. You do not find out what you meant when you said that Paris was the capital of France by examining introspectively the mental state you were in at the time.

Chapter Fourteen: The unconscious mind

Why have I so far failed to say anything about the fact that in modern society there is a class of professionals who take the mind as their province? They have university posts and degrees in the subject. They proclaim their subject to be a 'science'. Are not these the very people to tell us whether or not we have minds, and allay our doubts about it?

Alas, no. *Their* minds are already made up. This is so, regardless of whether they are diehard radical behaviourists (and believe that the mind is a verbal illusion) or not. The odd fact is that, as professionals, they ignore the question. Their main concerns – and very honourable ones – are either treating patients whose problems seem to be 'in the head' (as vulgar mindspeak would put it), or else advising people on matters concerning personal or public relations. Some even specialize in improving the performance of sportsmen, or training pets not to urinate on the living-room carpet. In a curious sense, psychology is the one profession where the existence or non-existence of the mind is – in practice – an irrelevance. Why would they need it, or need to debate it?

The only aspect of their professional activities on which I shall comment here is to observe that those who have taken it upon themselves to produce 'theories' of the mind have manifestly been in thrall to the language myth. The classic example is Sigmund Freud (1856-1939).

Freud's great achievement is usually claimed to be the discovery of the unconscious mind. It occasioned great excitement, because it seemed in one respect to undermine the traditional Western assumption that the human being was basically a rational creature. According to Freud, powerful forces were at work at an unconscious level, capable of overriding conscious rationality, or even – worse still – bending rationality to their own ends, unbeknown to the individual. Never was a more spiteful cat set among the philosophical pigeons.

It is sometimes said that Freud's account of the mind is just as unsatisfactory as Plato's account of matter, 'for they both invoke what they try to explain' (Gregory 1981: 355). But that is not my complaint here. I have no comment to make upon the details of the technical apparatus that Freud and his followers proceeded to construct in order to 'explain' the workings of the unconscious mind. It has nothing to do with vulgar mindspeak, except insofar as vulgar mindspeak may nowadays be open to accepting certain hackneyed expressions borrowed from psychoanalysis (the term *Freudian slip* might be one). What seems to me more significant is that Freud, whose clinical practice consisted mainly of listening to and talking to his patients, took over without question certain assumptions about speech already entrenched in the language myth.

The foremost of these is that linguistic communication is telementational, and that words represent 'ideas' in the mind of the speaker. Freud's great innovation to this model consisted in proposing that the process of expression might be far more devious than had hitherto been supposed. It could not be reduced to the simplistic assumption that speakers literally meant what they said. Indeed, they *did* mean what they said, but only indirectly and in a manner of which they themselves were not aware. It involved symbolism and a recondite kind of metaphor unrecognized by conventional linguists. Freud, I think, may be said to have embarked on an essentially linguistic inquiry, an investigation into what one of his followers later called 'the language proper of the unconscious' (Balogh 1971: 47). But that investigation, whether Freud realized it or not, was circumscribed in advance by his acceptance of part (at least) of the language myth concerning 'conscious' language.

It never occurs to Freud to question the notion that words are the manifestations of 'ideas': the only question is whether the manifestations are really what they seem to be.

> We know two things concerning our psyche or mental life: firstly, its bodily organ and scene of action, the brain (or nervous system), and secondly, our acts of consciousness, which are immediate data and cannot be more fully explained by any kind of description. Everything that lies between these two terminal points is unknown to us and, so far as we are aware, there is no direct relation between them. If it existed, it would at the most afford an exact localization of the processes of consciousness and would give us no help towards understanding them. (Freud 1949: 1)

It is interesting to see how the question of 'localizing' mental acts comes up here. This paragraph alone suffices to expose the intellectual straitjacket of Freud's inquiry. He sees the problem of 'mind' as being how to link up the brain with the 'immediate data' of consciousness. The 'brain' is one given – over here – and 'consciousness' – over there – is the other. He does not seem to appreciate that his two termini ('brain' and 'consciousness') do not belong to the same order of abstraction. No one whose thinking was not based on the language myth could fail to overlook this difference. It is as if one said: the problem of cricket is how to relate the immediate data of playing the game (scoring runs, taking wickets, etc.) with the physiological organ (the cricketer's body) that does these things. Nothing could be more preposterous: that is *not* the problem. There is no such problem. It only *seems* to be so if one has already been persuaded that there are two different kinds of cricketing phenomena involved, and that one kind is somehow causally dependent on the other.

A games theorist who set out to tackle the 'cricket problem' would be ridiculed mercilessly. But where the mind is concerned, the greatest respect is nowadays reserved for those, such as Freud, who spend their whole careers taking bogus problems seriously.

This is not to dismiss the experience of those who have benefited from treatment or advice given by Freudian psychoanalysts. But successful practice does not automatically validate dubious theory. Being cured of rheumatism by a course of Chinese acupuncture does not commit you to believing in *yin* and *yang*.

One thing the development of psychoanalytic theory did was give linguists a virtually unlimited field in which to conjure up further elaborations of the language myth. Under the aegis of the unfathomable 'unconscious', it became respectable to suppose that language was based on 'rules' that were not those found in traditional grammar books, but 'rules' buried deep in the mind below any possibility of awareness. Thus the grammarian could happily view a linguist's task as dealing not with what the linguistic community *thinks* it knows about its own language, but with 'mental processes that are far beyond the level of actual or even potential consciousness' (Chomsky 1965: 8). Chomsky's blank cheque was signed by Freud.

The notion of an unconscious mind was developed in a quite different direction by C.G. Jung (1885-1961) in his theory of the 'collective unconscious'. Jung drew attention to the similarities between recurrent images and symbols occurring in dreams, art and myths all over the world. These ubiquitous, pancultural patterns he called 'archetypes' and regarded as an inheritance from ancestral memory.

The unconscious mind is usually contrasted implicitly with the conscious mind as functioning in its 'normal' or everyday state. This in turn is to be distinguished from the mind when operating in what are nowadays termed 'altered states of consciousness'. These are usually taken to include dreaming, religious and hypnotic trance, and heightened awareness induced by drugs, deliberate deprivation of sensory stimuli, and programmes of mental and physical exercise (as in yoga). There is little, if any, agreement concerning the connexions between these 'altered states' and either the unconscious or the 'normal' conscious mind.

Perhaps the most dramatic evidence about the limitations of consciousness is provided by the work that has been done in psychology on subliminal perception. It now seems well established that I can 'take in' via the senses much more than I am aware of at the time, and act accordingly without my mind being involved at the level of consciousness at all. There has been considerable resistance to this idea, presumably because it 'seems to threaten notions of free will and personal autonomy' (Dixon 1987: 755). One of the most arresting manifestations is the phenomenon known as 'blindsight' (Weiskrantz 1986). This occurs in cases where damage to the brain prevents a person from 'seeing' what is visible to the eye, but nevertheless does not apparently interfere with identifying the location of objects in the visual field. Thus although the patient claims to be able to see nothing, it seems that the eye must be functioning effectively at some level below the threshold of consciousness. There are competing explanations of how this is possible, but that it takes place is not in doubt. For this reason, blindsight 'has often been seen as the ultimate litmus test for exploring conscious perception, allowing us to cross the Rubicon and investigate the mystery of consciousness' (Greenfield 2000: 77).

Whether it does, however, is doubtful. Some philosophers have objected to describing blindsight as if it entailed the existence of an internal monitoring system in the brain, distinct from the actual reception of optical stimuli and responsible for our subjective experience of seeing something (Bennett and Hacker 2003: 393-6). This makes no impression on those neurophysiologists who insist on asking 'Where is visual awareness generated?' (Rose 2006: 330-45). But do those who ask this question have any clear idea of what is being asked? It would be helpful, for a start, to know what could, in principle, 'generate' human awareness of *anything*. Blindsight and related phenomena already take us into areas of investigation that vulgar mindspeak was never designed to cope with. The 'generation' metaphor (if that is what it is) is no obvious improvement. It is symptomatic of the desperation that ensues when a certain programme of inquiry finds itself up against the current limits of language.

Chapter Fifteen: The conscious mind

The very term *unconscious mind* implies a contrast with *conscious mind*, suggesting that in order to understand the former we must first understand the latter. Unfortunately, there is no term in vulgar mindspeak more fiercely argued over than *consciousness* itself. During the heyday of behaviourism it had become a 'dirty word' to be banished from all scientific discussions of psychology, but even before the advent of behaviourism William James had written a provocative essay entitled 'Does consciousness exist?' (James 1904). Nowadays, by contrast, consciousness has been rehabilitated as one of the essential topics of psychological theory and philosophy of mind, as is indicated by the appearance of new academic series with such titles as *Consciousness and Cognition* and *Journal of Consciousness Studies*.

Some say that what is needed is a 'theory' of consciousness. Susan Blackmore, on the other hand, wonders whether a theory of consciousness is feasible, since 'the term is used in so many contradictory ways that it is hard to know what such a theory would have to accomplish' (Blackmore 1999: 237). This sentiment is echoed by Andy Clark, who observes that 'the word "consciousness" does not seem to aim at a single, steady target', so that it is unclear 'exactly what would *count* as a theory, sketch, story or explanation' (Clark 2001: 171). Max Velmans cheerfully introduces his book *Understanding Consciousness* with the admission that 'no universally agreed definition of the term "consciousness" exists' (Velmans 2000: 33). Susan Greenfield writes of consciousness: 'We all know what it is, yet it defies definition' (Greenfield 2000: 171).

Yet whether we do 'all know what it is' seems contradicted by the experts' disagreements among themselves. The experts, admittedly, have not made things easy, because they habitually wrap the topic up in oddly opaque descriptions. For instance, Daniel Dennett writes:

> Those things of which I am conscious, and the ways in which I am conscious of them, determine *what it is like to be me*. (Dennett 1987: 161. Italics in the original.)

I find it very difficult to understand what is being asserted here, because of this curious phrase *what it is like*. For me, being who and what I am is a notion that gives rise to no problem; but the question of 'what it is like' to be who and what I am, or even that 'kind' of person, does not make much sense. There isn't anything that being me is 'like', except being in various ways – I don't doubt – very much like many other people. But if the emphasis is supposed to fall on the *me*, it seems that I am being asked what makes me different from other people. And that seems an equally odd question. My eyesight is better than some people's, but worse than others. (It can be tested and compared if anyone is interested.) Likewise for my height, weight, average blood sugar level and reaction times. Like many others – but unlike many more – I prefer wine to beer, watching cricket to watching football, and so on, *ad infinitum*. What would be the point of listing all these particulars, and could such an account ever be completed? There is no mystery here, except one that has been gratuitously introduced by talking about 'what it is like'.

John Searle is another who worries about 'what it is like' to be himself. He assures us that 'there is definitely something that it feels like to be me' (Searle 2004: 205) and recommends that we try imagining what it was like to be Adolf Hitler, or Napoleon, or George Washington. I have tried all three, but to no avail: it did not help me understand what it is *like* to be me.

Even less am I tempted to try to imagine what it is like to be a bat (Nagel 1974), a question much discussed by philosophers. Insofar as drawing attention to this imaginative difficulty is meant simply to highlight the fact that everything science can tell us about bats still does not tell us much about the experience of life as a bat, I agree. But to conjure up from this a mysterious quality of 'what-its-likeness' (Papineau 2000: 15), allegedly characteristic of 'mental states', gets us nowhere.

The mystery has been fabricated by twisting a perfectly harmless idiom into an incomprehensible question. I can quite sensibly say that I do know or don't know what it is like to be starving, or fail an examination, be an Olympic athlete, etc., meaning either that I have had or not had these experiences, or that I think I can or cannot imagine having them. And someone *else* can, if so inclined, similarly wonder what it is like to be me. But transferring this into the first person and asking myself what it is like to be me is a linguistic move that invites suspicions of insanity. And in any case it has nothing to do with my understanding of my own conscious mind, as far as I can see.

This same 'what it is like ' idiom has been extended to cover the whole field of conscious perception. According to Jaegwon Kim, 'there is *something it is like*' to experience pains, itches, tickles, afterimages and anything else you might be conscious of.

> When you look at a green patch, there is a distinctive way the patch looks to you: It *looks green*, and your visual experience involves this green look. (Kim 2006: 15. Italics in the original.)

On this basis, philosophers have invented a whole realm of so-called 'qualia' to include 'these sensory, qualitative states, or the sensory qualities experienced in such states'

(Kim 2006: 15), and thus compounded the conceptual muddle. (Green is no longer just a colour, but the 'quale' that seeing green 'is like'.)

According to Bennett and Hacker, the experts have piled up confusions for themselves by unwarrantably stretching the concept of consciousness. Philosophers 'extend the concept of consciousness to encompass all perceptual experience and more.' In company with neuroscientists and cognitive scientists, they are 'inclined to equate consciousness with sentience in general, or indeed to extend it dramatically to almost the whole range of the mental' (Bennett and Hacker 2003: 263).

This will not do, in Bennett and Hacker's view, because for one thing there is no reason to suppose that when we perceive something we are conscious of it. Likewise, they argue, it is mistaken to suppose 'that whenever one is in a certain mental state, one must also be transitively conscious of so being' (Bennett and Hacker 2003: 263). They distinguish between 'transitive' and 'intransitive' consciousness: intransitive consciousness is just a matter of being conscious or awake, as opposed to being unconscious or asleep, whereas transitive consciousness is a matter of being conscious *of* something, or *that* something is or is not the case.

Their argument seems to depend a great deal on the everyday use of expressions like *to be conscious of* and to *be aware of*. (These do not, they claim, mean the same. On the contrary, 'whatever one is conscious of, one is also aware of, but one may be aware of things of which one is not conscious' (Bennett and Hacker 2003: 248).) Their examples are not always convincing. Thus 'one cannot be said to be either conscious or not conscious of one's wife as one sits chatting to her' (Bennett and Hacker 2003: 254n.34). But for many of us this would be a paradigm case of being conscious of someone: why else address your remarks to someone sitting in the same room? If the answer is that you can be aware of your wife's presence without being conscious of her, that begins to sound like hair-splitting.

It may be that some English speakers do make such a distinction between *I am aware of my wife sitting there* and *I am conscious of my wife sitting there*, but others certainly do not. (Bennett and Hacker do not seem to have done any serious linguistic research into the question.)

The same authors refuse to count having a dream as a conscious experience, or even an experience at all: 'to dream is not to have any experiences, although it may involve dreaming that one has experiences' (Bennett and Hacker 2003: 247n.25). But if one were not conscious of what seemed to be going on in one's dream world, it is difficult to see how one could report it on waking.

These disagreements serve to illustrate how difficult it is to find any consensus about the term *consciousness*. I shall return in Chapter Twenty-Four to Greenfield's contention that consciousness is undefinable. An even more pessimistic suggestion is sometimes made to the effect that the problem of consciousness will remain insoluble because the human mind lacks the concepts required to solve it. This seems to be the view of McGinn in his book *Consciousness and its Objects*. There he proposes that the problem is 'not one that we can solve with our current cognitive faculties' (McGinn 2004: 12). If that is so, sceptics are quick to retort, there is not much point in bothering one's mind about it (except for professional philosophers, who are paid to worry about insoluble problems).

Chapter Sixteen: The self-conscious mind

Many people suppose that the distinguishing mark of the mature human mind is not just consciousness but *self*-consciousness: 'we seem to differ from other animals and human infants in our ability to be massively self-conscious' (Greenfield 2000: 169).

> Self-awareness is very rare in the animal kingdom; only apes share with us the ability to recognize themselves in a mirror. But even they show no signs of being capable of insight, of introspection, of contemplating their future. Perhaps self-consciousness is an intense form of consciousness, requiring exceptionally large neuron assemblies and sophisticated brains. (Greenfield 2000: 185)

Psychiatrists have attached great importance to the 'mirror-phase' in the development of children. According to the French psychiatrist Jacques Lacan, who first identified it, infants between six and eighteen months show great fascination with their own image in a mirror, and this is the experience which lays the foundation for the recognition of the ego (Lacan 1949).

Self-consciousness is usually regarded as a precondition for developing some of the more advanced strategies of which human beings are capable, such as 'meta-memory':

The child or adult who has some awareness of the work-

ings of his or her own mind will make use of this knowledge in memorizing new materials. For example, new
information will be systematically categorized before
being committed to memory. This knowledge is com-
plemented by an awareness of the nature of forgetting,
so that external memory aids such as a diary or a knot
in a handkerchief come to be used as reminders. In both
examples, the ability to "reflect" upon the memory process enables the voluntary introduction of superordinate
monitoring and control processes. Other meta-mnemonic
processes include checking, planning, testing, revising
and evaluation. (Butterworth 1983: 394)

So what exactly is self-consciousness and how does it
relate to consciousness of any other kind? Bertrand Russell pointed out that the term *self-conscious* is potentially
misleading, because what we are conscious of in the first
instance is not a *self* (whatever that is) but just having
particular thoughts and feelings (Russell 1912: 50). We
cannot by introspection detect the 'I' who is having these
thoughts and feelings. Nevertheless, Russell thought that
self-consciousness was a special case of what he called
'knowledge by acquaintance', i.e. knowledge acquired by
direct perception 'without the intermediary of any process
of inference or any knowledge of truths' (Russell 1912:
46). For example, the colour, shape, hardness, smoothness,
etc. of the table now in front of us. This kind of knowledge
he held to be 'essentially simpler than any knowledge of
truths'.

Self-consciousness, according to Russell, is one of the
things that distinguish human beings from animals:

animals, we may suppose, though they have acquaintance with sense-data, never become aware of this acquaintance. I do not mean that they *doubt* whether they
exist, but that they have never become conscious of the
fact that they have sensations and feelings, nor therefore
of the fact that they, the subjects of their sensations and

feelings, exist. (Russell 1912: 49-50)

Russell's interpretation of self-consciousness as a form of knowledge by acquaintance has been taken up more recently by Colin McGinn, who holds that this is true of consciousness in general: 'we know what consciousness is by acquaintance' (McGinn 2004: 9). McGinn maintains further that, since this is so, 'we can just see that consciousness is not reducible to neural or functional processes', in just the same way as our acquaintance with the colour red tells us that red is not the same as green (McGinn 2004: 9).

There is a problem, however, both with Russell's position and with McGinn's. For the aspect of experience called 'self-consciousness' is radically unlike any other form of knowledge available to me (if indeed it is a form of knowledge at all). In my perception of the colour, shape, hardness, smoothness, etc. of a material object I am receiving impressions from 'outside', which is where the object seems to be; but the consciousness that *I* am the recipient of those impressions cannot come from anywhere 'outside', since my being the recipient is not an external object, or the property of any external object. Nor, *pace* McGinn, does my acquaintance with consciousness tell me that it is not reducible to neural or functional processes, any more than my visual acquaintance with the colours red and green already tells me that I am not dealing with light of the same wavelength. (That conclusion comes much later.)

So if self-consciousness is rightly regarded as a form of knowledge by acquaintance, it must be a quite different kind of 'acquaintance' from that which I have with anything in the external world.

An altogether different view of the matter is taken by those of the 'language first' persuasion, who relate self-consciousness (and much else) to linguistic competence. According to Bennett and Hacker, possession of a language 'extends the intellect':

self-consciousness is an ability which is available only to creatures that possess rich linguistic abilities. It is a consequence of the possession of sophisticated linguistic powers to use proper names and pronouns, as well as psychological predicates and predicates of action, in both the first- and third-person cases and in the various tenses [...].

Bennett and Hacker are quite adamant that what animals lack which makes them incapable of self-consciousness is not some special psychological insight into their own existence: what they lack is a language. In reply to the objection that 'putting language first' puts the cart before the horse, Bennett and Hacker insist that concepts have no priority over their linguistic expression. Rather, it is mastery of certain forms of linguistic expression that makes corresponding concepts available.

But there is a problem here too. This approach ignores the Lacanian 'mirror-phase', which seems to be negotiated without significant linguistic props of any kind. If Bennett and Hacker are right, English children cannot be self-conscious before the age when they have acquired the grammar of first-person pronouns, etc. From current studies of language acquisition, this seems highly implausible. It would also follow that if on Mars we found a race of intelligent Martians speaking a language that had neither pronouns nor proper names, they would have to be pronounced as lacking self-consciousness too, regardless of what their other cultural achievements were. And that seems just as implausible.

For Bennett and Hacker, being self-conscious is a *consequence* of linguistic accomplishments. (That is rather like saying that being middle-class is a *consequence* of owning a car, living in a certain suburb, etc.) The commonsense view is that, while it is true that self-consciousness may be manifested by, *inter alia*, demonstrating a mastery of certain forms of linguistic expression (such as first-person pronouns), that is only one criterion among others. It cannot be used to determine whether languageless creatures are self-conscious or not.

Other philosophers have tied themselves in knots over what are called 'higher order thoughts' (or HOTs, as the current philosophical jargon calls them). If you have a thought about something, it seems tempting to say that you must also be able to have a thought about *that* thought. (Thinking about where to go on holiday – the argument goes – is not to be confused with thinking about thinking about where to go on holiday. I can think, for example, that my thinking about going on holiday is a waste of time, even while thinking about it.) According to a leading HOT theorist, David Rosenthal, this relates to self-consciousness in the following way:

> Each HOT ascribes the state it is about to a particular self, and absent any countervailing reason, we take the self to which each HOT ascribes a state to be the same from one HOT to the next. [...] Because we interpret the self as being the same from one HOT to another, we are conscious of all our conscious states as belonging to the same self. (Rosenthal 2005: 17).

This tortuous explanation gets everything back-to-front. It is not *because* I attribute thoughts to the same thinker that I end up identifying myself as being that thinker. That would be like supposing that it was the experience of writing cheques and finding that the amount left in the bank diminished accordingly that led me eventually to realize that it was my own account that the money came from. Unless I were self-conscious in the first place, thinking about my own thoughts would make no sense at all.

Chapter Seventeen: The extraordinary mind

Genius is the popular mindspeak term for a person with remarkable intellectual abilities. But when these abilities extend to being able to multiply large numbers instantly and correctly, or recite long texts from memory after a single inspection, medical specialists begin to speak of 'syndromes' and 'conditions'. And when unusual abilities are accompanied by inability to perform simpler tasks which 'normal' minds take for granted, the genius has become a freak, an *idiot savant*.

The areas in which supernormal abilities emerge are varied: linguistic, mnemonic, artistic, musical and mathematical. Cardinal Mezzofanti, Vatican librarian in the early 19th century, could reportedly speak thirty-nine languages fluently. The infant Mozart is said to have been able to pick out chords on the keyboard at the age of three. Child prodigies are not exactly two a penny, but they are not uncommon either. Less well authenticated claims for mental powers involve recalling events that took place in a previous life, to say nothing of the vast body of publications dealing with the 'paranormal', the alleged ability of 'psychics' to communicate with people now dead, etc. The use of hypnosis to cure disorders was developed in the 19th century, and continues to some extent today, although it is not well understood and tends to be frowned on by the medical Establishment.

Even if we steer clear of the more controversial end

of this range of claims, there are plenty of puzzles in well verified cases. Individuals with extraordinary mental skills have been investigated seriously by psychologists since the early part of the 20th century. The Russian psychologist A.R. Luria, professor of psychology at Moscow University, studied the case of a man who could repeat long sequences of numbers and nonsense words with perfect accuracy after a single presentation, even years later (Luria 1968). Luria's subject could also reproduce such sequences in reverse order, and identify the item immediately preceding any one that the experimenter picked out at random. The clinical neurologist Oliver Sacks describes two twins who, when presented with any date from a period in the past or future 40,000 years, could immediately say what day of the week it was or would be. They could also state the date of Easter in any given year during the same period. On one occasion, a box of matches was accidentally spilt onto the floor, and the twins simultaneously cried out '111', which turned out to be exactly the number of matches that had fallen out. When asked by Sacks how they were able to count the matches so quickly, they replied that they had not counted, but simply 'saw' that there were 111 (Sacks 1965: 189). These twins, however, had low IQ and could not manage simple addition or subtraction with any accuracy, while multiplication and division were quite beyond them.

In trying to 'explain' such phenomena, drawing a distinction between the conscious and the unconscious mind does not help a great deal. Even if it is supposed that calculations of which the individuals are unaware go on in the unconscious mind, that still leaves the extraordinary rapidity and reliability of the process unaccounted for. If an unconscious algorithm is being applied for working out calendrical puzzles, experts still fail to understand how the algorithm was arrived at in the first place.

What conclusions can be drawn from such cases? It is tempting to suppose that if your brain were 'wired up' differently, you too could perform prodigious mental feats.

What is now treated as mental abnormality might be commonplace, and what is now regarded as normal might be present only in rare instances. In other words, there is no intrinsic scale of values where mental capacities are concerned. Feats regarded as easy and feats regarded as extraordinarily difficult are merely relative to what the majority of the human population seems to be able to do. The supernormal and the subnormal are not so different except when viewed from the middle ground that the majority comfortably occupy.

A more subtle but more controversial conclusion is brought out by Sacks. It concerns our notions of what is 'concrete' and what is 'abstract'. Patients who are commonly regarded as suffering from 'brain damage' or mental 'defects' of some kind are people who appear to live in a world which is 'vivid, intense, detailed, yet simple, precisely because it *is* concrete: neither complicated, diluted, nor unified, by abstraction'. It is often seen by neurologists as an impoverished world, lacking what the neurologists' own education has taught them to regard as supreme achievements of the human mind: complex categorization and 'propositional thought'. According to Sacks, this is an intellectual 'inversion' of the natural state of affairs, because the concrete is precisely 'what makes reality "real"' (Sacks 1965: 164).

Here there is a rapid slide from neurology into metaphysics. The slide is all the more alarming because what makes an experience real for someone is not a question that can be answered by peering into the cerebral cortex, any more than what 'explains' an Olympic record-breaking performance can be answered by inspecting the anatomy of the athlete's muscles.

Moreover, the genius sometimes seems to be gifted not with an ability to proceed to even higher levels of abstraction, but with the facility to grasp more simply and 'concretely' what for others are abstractions. This is clear from the remarkable autobiography of Daniel Tammet, who is both a 'lightning calculator' and synaesthesic. He is diagnosed as suffering from Asperger's syndrome. Tammet sees both numbers and letters of the alphabet in colour. He can calculate vast numbers 'in my head without any conscious effort'. He just 'sees' the answer as 'a distinctive visual pattern in my head'. He can draw schematic diagrams of numbers: 37 is 'lumpy like porridge', while 89 looks like falling snow. When he identifies a number as prime, he reports a sudden rush of feeling in the front centre of his head, 'like the sudden sensation of pins and needles'. The title of his book is *Born on a Blue Day*, which alludes to the fact that he was born on a Wednesday, and 'Wednesdays are always blue' (Tammet 2006).

For most people, Wednesdays are no particular colour, and the question 'What colour is your Wednesday?' does not make sense. According to some linguists, such a question would just not be 'grammatical' English. But if that is so, then there seems in principle to be no place to draw the line between linguistic sense and nonsense. Where the mind is concerned, one cannot even take 'grammar' for granted, let alone 'meaning'. Presumably if everyone saw Wednesdays as blue, then the expression *blue Wednesday* would be as tautological as *three-sided triangle*. Or can we be absolutely sure even of that?

Learning a foreign language, for Daniel Tammet, is ridiculously easy. He mastered Lithuanian from scratch in a few weeks, and could even be mistaken for a native speaker. He subsequently learnt Spanish, Rumanian and Welsh with no more difficulty. For those interested in the role of language in mental development, it is interesting to compare Tammet's story with that of Ildefonso, an impoverished Mexican immigrant to the United States, who had no language at all until the age of 27. The reason for Ildefonso's language problem was simply that he was born deaf and had no one to help him during his childhood. He was 'languageless' in the sense that he did not even grasp that the things he could see and touch had 'names' (either verbal or non-verbal). The account of how he eventually managed the breakthrough to language is told in Susan

Schaller's book *A Man Without Words* (Schaller 1991). It was due to her selfless dedication as a teacher.

Schaller describes the occasion on which, after endless frustrations, she managed to get Ildefonso to understand the connexion between the drawing of a cat on the blackboard and the (manual) sign 'cat':

> Suddenly he sat up, straight and rigid, his head back and his chin pointing forward. The whites of his eyes expanded as if in terror.
> [...] His head turned to his left and very gradually back to his right. Slowly at first, then hungrily, he took in everything as though he had never seen anything before: the door, the bulletin board, the chairs, tables, students, the clock, the green blackboard, and me. (Schaller 1991: 44)

And immediately he began to demand in dumb show that his teacher tell him what all these various things were 'called'.

For me, the moving description of this Eureka moment suffices to answer many questions about language and consciousness. I can see no ground for maintaining that, before the revelation of 'language', Ildefonso was not self-conscious and as well aware of his physical environment as his teacher. What he learnt when the penny finally dropped was not 'the concept cat', nor even one way of communicating 'about cats' to other people, but a whole new basis for integrating his world with theirs.

Chapter Eighteen: The tidy mind

Do you think any of your thoughts are complete? Or is thinking an amorphous, continuous process? A sentence was traditionally defined as an arrangement of words expressing a 'complete thought'. Hence ability to construct a grammatical sentence correctly (e.g. *The cat sat on the mat*, as opposed to, say *Cat the on mat sat the*) could itself be seen as evidence not only that you have a mind, but of the way the mind works (i.e. selecting from a range of smaller units and arranging them in a meaningful order to form tidy, self-contained wholes).

This naive idea survives in the work of the Russian psychologist Lev Vygotsky, who explicitly set out to tackle what he called 'one of the most complex problems of psychology, the interrelation of thought and language' (Vygotsky 1962: xix). Vygotsky is seen by his admirers as a psychologist who 'would not brook either materialist reductionism or mentalism, nor the easy Cartesian dualism that opted frontally for one and let the other in through the back door' (Bruner 1962: vi). But on closer examination we see that, as in Freud's case, aspects of his theorizing are based upon an uncritical acceptance of the language myth.

Vygotsky's initial premise is that 'the primary function of speech is communication' (Vygotsky 1962: 6, 19). His account of communication is overtly telementational. Language is necessary because 'direct communication between minds is impossible [...]. Thought must pass first through meanings and then through words' (Vygotsky 1962: 150). Mature verbal communication is aimed at 'an understanding between minds', made possible by 'mediation' through a 'system of signs' (Vygotsky 1962: 6). He speaks of 'communicating' thoughts, and his account of the process by which thoughts come to be expressed in the act of speech bears obvious comparison with Saussure's: there is a sequence, beginning with the pure thought, which is then shaped in pre-verbal 'inner speech', next in word-meanings, and finally in words (Vygotsky 1962: 152).

Vygotskyan mindspeak thus distinguishes four main phases in the process. He differs from Saussure principally in taking as his point of departure a phase in which the 'thought' has no linguistic shape at all, and then tracing the way in which it is gradually differentiated and linearized.

> When I wish to communicate the thought that today I saw a barefoot boy in a blue shirt running down the street, I do not see every item separately: the boy, the shirt, its blue color, his running, the absence of shoes. I conceive of all this in one thought, but I put it into separate words. A speaker often takes several minutes to disclose one thought. In his mind the whole thought is present at once, but in speech it has to be developed successively. (Vygotsky 1962: 150)

One of the problems with this account of the process is that it is difficult to see how anything as totally undifferentiated as Vygotsky's initial unit could reasonably be called a 'thought' at all. In what kind of whole do the parts have no separate identities or locations? Picking out the boy, the shirt, the bare feet, etc. already presupposes some kind of analysis, some focussing of attention; as in the case of visual experience, the simultaneous grasping of a complex does not require starting from an initial blur in which everything was all rolled into one. Furthermore, it is no coincidence that the 'thought' is then characterized by precisely those features that eventually emerge in an identifiable verbal guise. If we ask, for instance, whether the boy in the blue shirt was wearing a hat, there is no answer. But when Vygotsky saw him, he must either have had a hat or not had a hat. Did Vygotsky not notice? Or was that detail deliberately excluded from the 'thought' that found verbal expression in a sentence? Presumably its inclusion would have yielded a different 'thought' from the one Vygotsky describes. But how can one distinguish one thought from another at the stage where they all start life as amorphous, featureless mental items? It seems that only when I inspect the resultant sentence can I tell exactly what my initial thought was in the first place. In short, the identity and individuation of thoughts becomes apparent only in retrospect, thanks to language. This is rather like proposing a theory of travel in which it is supposed that your itinerary and destination can be identified only *after* the journey has been concluded.

The difficulty is obvious in the case of numbers. If, counting the words in a sentence, or the vacant seats in a room, I announce the total as 'forty-nine', did I actually start that speech act with an undifferentiated numerical thought, which only gradually emerged (via 'inner speech' and then 'word meanings') as having the numerical structure that differentiates it from the thought 'fifty'? I cannot by introspection detect any such progression. (*A*: 'Have you counted the total yet?' *B*: 'Yes, I have.' *A*: 'Tell me what it is.' *B*: 'I can't. My mind hasn't put it into words yet.')

It should be noted that inner speech, for Vygotsky, is not a silent echo or rehearsal of spoken sounds. Nor does it involve incipient activation of the vocal cords. That would be too close to the behaviourist position.

> Inner speech is not the interior aspect of external speech – it is a function in itself. [...] Inner speech is to a large extent thinking in pure meanings. It is a dynamic, shifting, unstable thing, fluttering between word and thought

[...]. (Vygotsky 1962: 149)

Nevertheless, although strictly pre-verbal, inner speech has its own syntax, according to Vygotsky. There are sentences, but marked by the predominance of predicates and the omission of subjects (Vygotsky 1962: 139). For Saussure, none of this would have made any sense at all: there is no such activity as 'thinking in pure meanings' because meanings are meanings *of words*. A meaning cannot be a meaning of nothing, i.e. exist as an autonomous mental entity, any more than an economic value can be a value of nothing. Meanings, for Saussure, are not present in the mind in any abstract state divorced from their corresponding *images acoustiques*. For Vygotsky, on the other hand, word-meanings make their appearance only at the stage *after* 'inner speech': 'inner speech' is not yet 'verbal thought'. Word-meanings (but not yet actual word-forms) are needed to transform 'inner speech' into 'verbal thought'. It is 'in word meaning that thought and speech unite into verbal thought' (Vygotsky 1962: 5).

It is not difficult to spot what is going wrong here. Vygotsky has begun by identifying a series of increasingly abstract points of view from which a given sentence might be considered. 1. The most abstract stage is considering the sentence as a single unanalysed, independent grammatical unit (call it U), several of which may be concatenated to form a discourse ($U1 + U2 + U3 + U4...$). 2. At a less abstract level, this single unit (U) can be divided into parts, e.g. corresponding to what traditional grammarians called subject and predicate ($S + P$). 3. At a less abstract level still, both these parts can be given a general function: e.g. 'actor' + 'action'. 4. Finally, at the least abstract level, the individual words can be specified, e.g. *Dogs* (subject) + *bark* (predicate).

There is nothing wrong with any of these separate ways of considering a sentence, and each may be useful for different purposes. The mistake – Vygotsky's mistake – consists in stringing them all together and treating them as actual successive psychological phases in the production of a speech act ($U > S + P >$ 'actor' + 'action' $> dogs + bark$). In this way what was originally designed to serve the purposes of Greek grammarians and logicians ends up in the hands of the psychologist as a theory of what goes on in the mind every time we speak.

This is not plausible evidence of inner processes at work but a speculative conflation of different levels of external analysis.

Chapter Nineteen: The integrated mind

In Chapter Seven I promised a more plausible account of human communication than the telementational model. Here it is. I call it an 'integrational' model.

Try the following experiment. Keep a log of *all* the occasions in daily life on which you speak to other people. I think you will observe after a while that the vast majority of them are occasions on which you are trying to integrate your own activities with theirs, or they are trying to integrate their activities with yours. In short, you are constantly engaged in patterns of activity which the parties involved are endeavouring to influence in one way or another, whether to make certain things happen, or stop them happening, speed them up, or facilitate or modify them. These patterns of activity commonly involve familiar physical objects of some kind – chairs, tables, items of food and clothing, knives, forks, motor cars, television sets and all the rest of the equipment for daily living with which human beings surround themselves.

I think you will also observe that very rarely do you supply or ask for information 'for its own sake'. If you ask what the time is, or where the bus station is, or what the annual rainfall in Adelaide is, it is usually because you have some programme to which this information is relevant; and you seldom offer such items of information spontaneously to others – although you could quite easily do so – unless you have reason to suppose that *they* have a programme where it would be useful to know such things. The social world is not one in which people go around non-stop making gratuitous announcements of what they happen to know; and anyone who habitually did that would be treated as needing medical help of some kind.

If you pay careful attention to the everyday occasions on which you speak to others I would be surprised if you did not notice that very rarely does verbal communication go unaccompanied by non-verbal communication. On the contrary, the two are closely integrated. Facial expressions, gestures, gaze and bodily posture are constantly brought into play, being integrated both with speech and with the execution of other activities, such as holding objects or moving them from one place to another, sitting down, standing up, and so on. Communication, in short, involves a continuum of activities, in which the role of words varies from case to case. On occasions where non-verbal communication is strictly curtailed – as in a telephone conversation, where you cannot see the person you are talking to – it is noticeable how words have to take on extra duties, or else how limited the range of topics becomes.

By far the most crucial aspect of everyday communication, however, is identification of *who it is* you are interacting with. In most cases this too is effected non-verbally. You recognize the individuals involved (your wife does not have to say every day 'Good morning, I am your wife'), or you make inferences about them on the basis of what they are doing, how they are dressed, and the circumstances in which you encounter them. All this influences both *what* you say, *how* you say it, and – no less importantly – what you do *not* say (because it would be superfluous, inappropriate, indiscreet, etc.).

Without going any further, I think the factors mentioned so far should be enough to persuade you that there is something very odd, to say the least, about any theory of language which starts from the assumption that the main purpose of words is to express ideas – ideas being otherwise incommunicable abstractions that for some reason one wishes to share with others. Nothing of the kind fits the scenario you find when you examine the commonplace uses of language. Words are in the first instance tools for living. The idea that they are primarily tools for *thinking* is a prejudice derived from the way we have been educated; and in particular – in my view – from the fact that our society has educational institutions that give priority to written texts and abilities associated with writing.

Living, if I am right, is a process of integration, and I have so far mentioned three of the kinds of integration involved. One is the integration of one's own activities with those of others. Another is the integration of those activities with the physical world in which we all have to find – if we can – food and shelter sufficient to sustain ourselves and our families from day to day. A third is the integration of verbal with non-verbal communication.

I am inclined to believe that none of us would be able to master the rudiments of verbal communication were it not that in the normal course of events our initial needs are met by non-verbal communication. I am referring here to the kind of communication that takes place between mother and baby in the early weeks and months of life. It is into an initial matrix of non-verbal communication that verbal communication is gradually introduced, or, as I would prefer to say, integrated. Even in the case of an Ildefonso, whose extraordinary story I mentioned in Chapter Seventeen, it was necessary to have a framework of non-verbal communication into which the first 'names' of things could be slotted. In other words, my thesis is that integration between various modes of communication is not only a permanent feature of our adult lives, but is essential for the development of language in the first place.

There is a fourth mode of integration that is tacitly implied in all of this, but which I have not so far mentioned. Everything we do as human beings involves the integration of the present with the past and the future: this is temporal integration. The past we can only remember and the future we can only anticipate. But unless we could

relate the here-and-now to both of these, our lives would
not be those of human beings. To convince oneself of this,
it suffices to try to imagine ('try' because it is not actually
imaginable) that you immediately forgot – permanently –
whatever you were doing a second ago, and were unable
to anticipate in any way what might happen in the next few
seconds or subsequently. If that were the case, you could
have no grasp of time. And without that you would not be
a human being.

These considerations suffice to convince me that a vi-
able approach to language will have to have as its basic
premise that human beings communicate with one another
not by exchanging thoughts but by integrating their many
activities. This is not – please note – to deny that human
beings think. But languages are not systems for the expression of thoughts: the essential function of words is the con-
textualized integration of activities. From that integration
come what are called the 'meanings' not only of words
but of the many varieties of non-verbal signs that human
beings have developed. Describing the meaning of a word
(as dictionaries do) is not identifying a concept mysteri-
ously attached to it, but giving a shorthand account of how
its use can be integrated with that of other words.

Realizing this makes a great difference to how you approach questions concerning 'the mind'. The mind, seen
in this perspective, is the creation of mindspeak, and if
you wish to understand when people are talking sense or
nonsense about the mind you must first understand what
mindspeak is for. I shall come back to this shortly, after
exploring some possible non-integrationist views of the
mind.

A roundabout confirmation of what I have been saying
above seems to me to be provided by what Einstein did
when he rejected Newton's conception of absolute time
and provided a new way of pinning down 'simultaneity' in
physics. Einstein pointed out that it was of no help to the
physicist to look up the word *simultaneous* in a dictionary, only to find that it meant 'at the same time'. What the

physicist wants to know is what *at the same time* means. Einstein proposed that in order to determine whether or not two events far apart take place at the same time, what is needed is an observation station at the mid point of a straight line between the two, and an arrangement of mirrors allowing both events to be seen without shifting the gaze.

Einstein's proposal encountered the obvious objection that this will not work unless there is some assurance that light travels to the observer from one event at the same speed as it does over the same distance from the other event. And how could the physicist be sure of that without *already* having a way of measuring time? Einstein's answer to the objection is this. The requirement that light travel at the same speed over both distances is 'in reality neither a *supposition nor a hypothesis* about the physical nature of light, but a *stipulation*' made by the physicist (Einstein 1952: 23. Italics in the original).

In other words, Einstein realized that progress in physics depended on somehow integrating the terminology of science systematically with the activities of measurement that lay within the capacity of the scientist. Nothing more was possible and nothing less would do. That integrational model of meaning is the cornerstone of Einstein's theory of relativity.

Chapter Twenty: The cosmic mind

You may perhaps think you have a mind because you believe that everything in the universe has a mind of some
kind. (So it would be unreasonable to suppose that you
were the sole exception.)

I don't myself know anyone who reasons in this way
about their own mind, but I do know that many have believed that the whole universe, including its apparently
inert and inanimate bits, is alive. This doctrine is sometimes known as *hylozoism* (a term apparently coined by
the 17th-century English philosopher Ralph Cudworth) or
panpsychism. It is still debated by philosophers. According to David Chalmers in his book *The Conscious Mind*,
the possibility that not only is consciousness ubiquitous,
but experience too, cannot be dismissed (Chalmers 1996:
293). For John Searle, on the other hand, in *The Mystery
of Consciousness*, panpsychism is 'absurd' (Searle 1997:
156).

Alfred Russel Wallace, co-founder with Darwin of
modern evolutionary biology, maintained that the universe
must be the work of an infinitely intelligent supermind,
because the mathematical odds against the emergence of
the human race being the result of chance are incalcula-
bly vast (Wallace 1903). This is a development of what is
traditionally called the 'argument from design'. One of its
best known forms was the famous 'watch-maker' analogy
presented a century earlier by William Paley in his *Natu-*

ral Theology. (The analogy itself pre-dates Paley's use of it.) Here complexity of physical structure is taken as evidence of deliberate design, and hence the existence of a designer (Paley 1802). Similar arguments are nowadays advanced by creationists who reject Darwinian evolution. But all these beg the ontological question of whether mind or minds (whether of the cosmic, the superhuman or the personal variety) can exist independently of matter.

I do know that there are some people who believe on the basis of personal experience they are in contact with a mind or minds in outer space, and even more who believe that (some) human minds on earth can communicate to one another directly by means of telepathy. I have heard it maintained that the whole universe is a thought in the mind of God, but I do not know what to say about that because I am not sure what it is supposed to mean. I am not sure either what to say about the cosmic mind, because again I find it difficult to be sure I understand what it is supposed to be or do.

Richard Gregory, in his impressive book *Mind in Science*, credits the Greek philosopher Anaxagoras (500-428 BC) with being the first thinker to distinguish clearly between mind and matter. That is a good place to start, because it is hard to see how a discussion of anything to do with mind can get off the ground until mind is contrasted with *something else that is not mental*. Matter seems nowadays an obvious candidate for the non-mental slot. But how obvious that would have seemed to the contemporaries of Anaxagoras must not be taken for granted.

It is worth examining in detail the passage from Anaxagoras that Gregory cites and seeing just how the distinction is drawn.

> All other things have a portion of everything, but Mind is infinite and self-ruled, and is mixed with nothing but is all alone by itself. For if it was not by itself, but was mixed with anything else, it would have a share of all things if it were mixed with any; for in everything there

is a portion of everything, as I said earlier; and the things that were mingled with it would hinder it so that it could control nothing in the same way as it does now being alone by itself. For it is the finest of all things and the purest, it has all knowledge about everything and the greatest power; and Mind controls all things, both the greater and the smaller, that have life. Mind controlled also the whole rotation, so that it began to rotate in the beginning. And it began to rotate first from a small area, but it now rotates over a wider and will rotate over a wider area still. And the things that are mingled and separated and divided off, all are known by Mind. [...] Mind arranged them all, including this rotation in which are now rotating the stars, the sun and moon, the air and the aether that are being separated off. And this rotation caused the separating off. And the dense is separated off from the rare, the hot from the cold, the bright from the dark and the dry from the moist. But there are many portions of many things, and nothing is altogether separated off nor divided one from the other except Mind. (Gregory 1981: 24)

The passage in question actually comes second-hand from Simplicius (Kirk, Raven and Schofield 1983: 362-3) and the Greek word here translated as 'Mind' is *nous*. The distinction Anaxagoras wants to draw, as the passage quoted shows, is evidently tied up with speculation about the beginnings of the cosmos, and although it is not free of obscurities, one can say with some assurance that whatever Anaxagoras meant by *nous*, he conceived of it as an autonomous force or agency that originally set the universe in (circular) motion.

It seems, then, that what he was postulating as *nous* was defined basically by its role as a non-material agent controlling matter. This is its only positive attribute. If so, using the English term *mind* to identify it seems to me potentially misleading and elucidates nothing. (This is not to suggest that I have any better translation to offer. I would be inclined to say that in this context *nous* is untranslatable.)

It seems unlikely that Anaxagoras' story of how the universe began reflected the popular *nous*-speak of his day and age. On the contrary, he seems to be elevating the common word *nous* to the status of a technical term in his own cosmology, i.e. assigning to *nous* a theoretical role that it had not had before. This is confirmed by the severe criticism to which it is subjected in Plato's *Phaedo*. There Socrates recounts how eagerly he devoured the writings of Anaxagoras in order to learn exactly how the universe was controlled by *nous*, only to discover that Anaxagoras never assigned to it

> any responsibility for the management of things, but mentioned as causes air and ether and water and many other strange things. That seemed to me much like saying that Socrates' actions are all due to his mind, and then, in trying to tell the causes of everything I do, to say that the reason I am sitting here is because my body consists of bones and sinews, because the bones are hard and are separated by joints, that the sinews are such as to contract and relax, that they surround the bones along with flesh and skin which hold them together, then as the bones are hanging in their sockets, the relaxation and contraction of the sinews enable me to bend my limbs, and that is the cause of my sitting here with my limbs bent. (*Phaedo* 98)

In short, Socrates' objection is that it is no use postulating some non-material agency as a cosmic prime mover unless you are prepared to demonstrate in detail exactly how it is able to affect happenings in the material world. But more interesting than that, in the present context, is the actual example Socrates gives to support his objection. It strongly suggests that what comes most readily to hand as a test case is that of a man *deciding* to do something and then doing it. What is needed is an account of *that* connexion, not an account of the physical and physiological aspects of his implementing the decision.

> If someone said that without bones and sinews and all
> such things, I should not be able to do what I decided, he
> would be right, but surely to say that they are the cause
> of what I do, and not that I have chosen the best course,
> even though I act with my mind, is to speak very lazily
> and carelessly. (*Phaedo* 99a)

This may be the first example on record of an 'ordinary language' argument involving the mind and mindspeak. Manifestly, the same would apply to Socrates *deciding* to tell Cebes something and then actually *telling* him. The connexion is not explained by describing in detail the movements of Socrates' vocal organs or the sounds they make.

More interesting still is that Socrates' argumentative strategy involves invoking the existence of a personal mind in order to rebut a doctrine of the cosmic mind. In effect, Socrates is saying: 'If you can't even explain how *nous* manages to bring about our individual actions in everyday circumstances, like my sitting here and talking to you, it is absurd to appeal to the same agency as being in charge of the whole universe.'

I think Socrates hits the nail on the head there. I find it difficult to imagine that anyone would believe in a cosmic mind unless they *first* believed that they themselves, as individuals, had a mind. The doctrine of a cosmic mind, it seems to me, is an extrapolation from belief in a personal mind, and anyone who had to appeal to a cosmic mind in order to be sure of the existence or his or her own mind would be standing psychology on its head.

Chapter Twenty-One: The collective mind

More widespread nowadays than any doctrine of the cosmic mind is the belief that collectivities have minds of their own. That is to say, certain groups of human beings, by reason of their social or political status, or because of their physiological constitution, or some combination of these factors, think in a way that is typically different from the way other groups think. Thus we hear of, for example, 'the Chinese mind', 'the female mind', 'the military mind', 'the academic mind' and many more such 'minds'. In this usage the terms *mind* and *mentality* tend to be interchangeable.

The collective mind is perhaps most frequently invoked in connexion with foreigners: what distinguishes 'them' from 'us' is that they don't think like we do.

This goes back a long way. The belief that the Greek mind was different from (and superior to) that of other peoples predates Aristotle. It is implicit in the Classical view of 'the barbarian', which may be seen as underlying the historian Herodotus' descriptions of the exotic customs and practices of such peoples as the Persians, Egyptians and Scythians.

Apart from a lack of competence in Greek [...], the barbarian's defining feature is an absence of the moral responsibility required to exercise political freedom: the two are connected, since both imply a lack of *logos*, the

ability to reason and speak (sc. Greek) characteristic of
the adult male citizen. (Wiedemann 1996: 233)

The barbarians' lack of *logos* can thus be seen as explaining their un-Greek practices and beliefs, as well as
providing a reason why these outlandish practices and beliefs are hardly worthy of serious study. In addition, it of-
fers a justification for the theory of natural slavery that we
find in Aristotle (the demographic fact being that the great
majority of slaves in the Greek world were barbarians).

By late antiquity a different distinction between 'us'
and 'them' was in place. This was the religious distinction between the Christian mind and the pagan mind – a
distinction no less prejudicial to genuine understanding of
other societies, and one which remained so for centuries. A
view of the world in which the two most important events
were the Fall of Adam and the birth of Jesus is hardly con-
ducive to investigating the ignorant minds of those who
have never heard of either. Nor does the assumption that
a Christian's duty is to convert the heathen from their pagan ways, and as soon as possible, provide an encouraging
introduction to patient and tolerant inquiry into whether
'they' actually have different minds from 'ours'. On the
contrary, the elimination of misguided beliefs and practices becomes a priority. Romantic idealizations of the 'noble
savage', unsullied by civilization, played no part in the traditional programme of missionary Christianity.

From the Greeks onward, it is notable how often a perception of 'their' different mind is associated with a perception of how different 'their' language is. In the 19th
century, the theologian and philologist Richard Chenevix
Trench, later Archbishop of Dublin, declared: 'Language
is as truly on one side the limit and restraint of thought, as
on the other side that which feeds and unfolds it'. He sym-
pathized with those missionaries who complained of the
difficulty of their task because 'the very terms are wholly or nearly wholly wanting in the dialect of the savage
whereby to impart to him heavenly truths, or indeed even

the nobler emotions of the human heart.' In his view, 'as there is no such witness to the degradation of the savage as the brutal poverty of his language, so there is nothing that so effectually tends to keep him in the depths to which he has fallen' (Trench 1851: 19).

Leaving aside the stern disapproval of the savages and their linguistic insulation from heavenly truths, we see here an equation that has, in more erudite hands, survived to this day: between 'their' language and the way 'their' mind works.

The most fashionable version of the 'us' versus 'them' dichotomy in recent times has been 'male' versus 'female'. Linguistic differences between men and women have attracted the attention of linguists at least since the chapter on 'The Woman' in Otto Jespersen's *Language. Its Nature, Development and Origin* (1922). Jespersen attributed some of these differences to mental traits, although not always on the most convincing of evidence. He claimed:

> The greater rapidity of female thought is shown linguistically, among other things, by the frequency with which a woman will use a pronoun like *he* or *she*, not of the person last mentioned, but of somebody else to whom her thoughts have already wandered, while a man with his slower intellect will think that she is still moving on the same path. (Jespersen 1922: 252)

More recently, feminist theorists have fastened upon language not only as providing the evidence that male attitudes have condemned women to an inferior role in society, but on language reform as a way of changing those attitudes. This has been in full swing now at least since the publication in 1975 of Robin Lakoff's *Language and Woman's Place*, subsequently criticized from a feminist perspective in Dale Spender's polemic *Man Made Language*. According to Spender (a non-linguist), Lakoff (a linguist) had been guilty of accepting 'some of the sexist assumptions of the linguistic paradigm in which she worked' (Spender 1980: 8). She had accepted that there was something different about women's language which reflected various alleged psychological characteristics of women, including lack of conviction and lack of confidence, thus building up a picture of women as being 'deficient'.

Two things are interesting about this and similar controversies. One is the great readiness with which characteristics of the way a person uses words are interpreted as psychological indicators and given psychological labels, usually drawn from vulgar mindspeak. There is a standing assumption not only that *language reveals the mind* but that *linguistic differences between the sexes reflect mental differences between the sexes*. This kind of linguistic psychology actually drives the debate and is essential to it, for a very simple reason. If linguistic differences between men and women were 'merely verbal', they would be of no more significance than the fact that men's clothes button up left-over-right, whereas women's clothes button up the opposite way. Documenting differences as such would be of no interest, except perhaps to linguists. But such differences have to be interpreted psychologically as communicational breakdown, as in the title of Deborah Tannen's book on the subject, *You Just Don't Understand* (1990), which describes numerous cases of men and women talking at cross-purposes.

The other point of interest is how these assumptions in turn derive from acceptance of the language myth. Spender, for example, describes language as being not merely 'a vehicle which carries ideas' but itself 'a shaper of ideas'. It is 'the programme for mental activity' (Spender 1980: 139). From this it would follow that if the same words do not carry the same ideas for men as for women, the 'programmes for mental activity' of these two groups must differ. So just as in the case of Archbishop Trench, although in quite a different field, language is seen as simultaneously restricting and nourishing the mental outlook of particular collectivities.

Related assumptions underlie the ongoing debate about 'political correctness'. A recent definition of this phenomenon describes it as 'attempts to provide alternative forms of expression for those that serve to exclude, insult or marginalise less powerful groups within society' (Swann, Deumert, Lillis and Mesthrie 2004: 243). Examples given include the recommendation of *disabled* in preference to *crippled*.

The rationale of political correctness is nothing if not paradoxical. It presupposes that there is a collectivity of persons who do not think of themselves as being, or resent being thought of as – say, crippled – although that is in fact what they are. So the collectivity of non-cripples owes it to this minority to stop using the word *crippled* and use another word – e.g. *disabled* – instead. If successful, this strategy would presumably result in the obsolescence of the word *crippled* and its replacement by *disabled*. But that would simply result – as regularly in cases of euphemism – in transferring the meaning of the derogatory word to its substitute. What long-term benefit this brings to the crippled/disabled it is difficult to see. What is clear, on the other hand, is the crude assumption that words *determine* the mental horizons and attitudes of their users.

That this role of language *vis-à-vis* the mind is not just a possibility but a fact has found its strongest support in modern anthropology, to which I turn next.

Chapter Twenty-Two: The primitive mind

Is your mind (if you have one) basically any different from the mind of a hunter-gatherer living ten thousand years ago? The doctrine of the primitive mind, in its crudest form, tells us that primitive societies have always had ways of thinking that are quite different from 'ours'. This belief has never been confined to popular opinion among the uneducated, but was common among scholarly anthropologists of the 19th and early 20th centuries.

> This is explicit in the common use of the terms 'higher' and 'lower' races. Since it was taken for granted that the highest standards in knowledge, morals, and religion were at that time to be found among the educated classes of Europe and America, it was inferred that the converse of those standards must have been those of our earliest ancestors, of whom some living primitive tribes were thought to be the lingering survivals. (Lienhardt 1966: 9-10)

The doctrine of the primitive mind was bound up with acceptance of Darwinian evolution. It was supposed that the mind had gradually *evolved* to reach its present state (and was doubtless still evolving). In more recent times, far from dying down, the issue has acquired political overtones and become enmeshed in arguments about racism, ethnocentricity and 'political correctness'. With these associations, the doctrine has been for a long time in bad odour in intellectual circles. It is often seen as an unacceptable face of anthropology, a blot on the record of an otherwise praiseworthy discipline.

But this confuses the issue. If you are convinced you have a mind, you should be prepared to ask: 'Does it supply me with the same mental equipment as the mind of someone born into a quite different ethnic group and culture?' That question cannot be settled by a blank refusal to consider it.

So what is the evidence for the primitive mind? What are its characteristics held to be?

Darwin's French contemporary Auguste Comte, one of the founders of modern sociology, had no hesitation in describing it. He distinguished between three successive phases in the evolution of human thinking. The earliest he labelled 'theological': in this phase, he said, 'the human mind is not yet up to tackling the simplest of scientific problems' (Comte 1844: 56).

Darwin himself thought it incontrovertible that (1) 'all civilised nations are the descendants of barbarians', as shown by 'clear traces of their former low condition in still-existing customs, beliefs, language, etc.' and (2) 'savages are independently able to raise themselves a few steps in the scale of civilisation, and have actually thus risen' (Darwin 1874: 221). He postulated a continuum of mental advancement, stretching back in unbroken succession across races and species, and claimed that

> the difference in mind between man and the higher animals, great as it is, certainly is one of degree and not of kind. (Darwin 1874: 193)

And even more specifically:

> the mental powers of the higher animals, which are the same in kind with those of man, though so different in degree, are capable of advancement. Thus the interval

between the mental powers of one of the higher apes and
of a fish, or between those of an ant and scale-insect is
immense; yet their development does not offer any special difficulty. (Darwin 1874: 931)

In the perspective of Darwinian gradualism, the primitive mind stands on the intellectual threshold where some
primates develop a specifically human view of their own
existence and capacities.

That does not tell us a great deal about what the primitive mind can or cannot do. But one specific and highly
controversial claim was made by the French scholar Lu-
cien Lévy-Bruhl in his book *Les fonctions mentales dans
les sociétés inférieures* (1910), translated into English as
How Natives Think. It has continued to be a focus of debate ever since. This was the claim that the primitive mind
is 'pre-logical'. According to Lévy-Bruhl: 'Primitives see
with eyes like ours, but they do not perceive with the same
minds' (Lévy-Bruhl 1910: 44). Lévy-Bruhl backed this up
by reference to many examples of apparently 'pre-logical'
beliefs common among primitive peoples; for example, the
Australian aboriginal belief that the sun is a white cockatoo. Could any rational mind really believe that?

Lévy-Bruhl's critics disputed this kind of 'evidence'.
They argued that it was fallacious to apply Western stand-
ards of rationality to non-Western belief systems. The Eu-
ropean anthropologist who condemns the belief that the
sun is a white cockatoo as pre-logical can only reach this
conclusion by treating the aboriginal words for 'white
cockatoo' and 'sun' as having the same meanings as their
English translations have in English. But patently, for the
aboriginal speaker, they do not: being a white cockatoo
and being a radiant celestial body are not, for the aborigi-
ne, mutually exclusive possibilities. So Lévy-Bruhl's case
collapses by begging the question.

The problem with arguing against Lévy-Bruhl along
these lines is that the exchange soon reaches an uneasy
stalemate. By attacking Lévy-Bruhl in this way, the critics

are themselves doing exactly what they accuse Lévy-Bruhl of doing, i.e. arguing on the basis of 'Western' reasoning. So the score seems to be, at best, nil-nil. But is it even a draw? Defenders of Lévy-Bruhl might reply that this actually concedes Lévy-Bruhl's point: i.e. the primitive mind works in a way that is not amenable to judgment by Western reasoning. The critics have scored an own-goal, but without realizing it.

This is indirectly related to another question that has been the focus of controversy: is it possible for the human mind to think an impossible thought? Cognobabble here lapses into talking about 'possible worlds'. But that does not get us very far; for it is quite unclear whether a world in which *ex hypothesi* the sun is a white cockatoo counts as a possible world or not. Could there be such a world? Invoking a distinction between empirical and logical possibilities does not help much either; for the whole issue hinges on whose 'logic' is accepted. According to Kim, arguments based on the notion of possible worlds have to conform to a principle called 'necessity of identities'. This principle lays down that if X is the same as Y (as, for instance, Tully being the same person as Cicero), then X is *necessarily* Y: that is, X is the same as Y in every possible world (Kim 2006 : 39). We cannot have a world in which Cicero is tall and thin but Tully is short and fat.

By parity of reasoning, we cannot have a possible world in which the sun is a radiant heavenly body and at the same time a white cockatoo (granted that – to mention only two properties – the sun has no wings and a white cockatoo does not have the requisite energy to heat Australia). Yet the aboriginal belief apparently defies this possibility. So does the aboriginal mind make it possible to believe something that actually is an impossibility (and not just an impossibility for us)? Or, alternatively, are the aborigines mistaken about what they think they believe?

The necessity of identities does not come to the rescue here either. For it can be applied in favour of the aborigines. If for X we substitute the name of the sun and for Y the name of the white cockatoo, and if the two are the same, then – just as in the case of Tully and Cicero – they are necessarily the same, i.e. the same in all possible worlds. To believe that we live in a world where, as a matter of fact, the sun is not a white cockatoo, is to believe an impossibility. Or else to be mistaken about one's own belief. Neither conclusion, it goes without saying, is welcome to Western philosophers and psychologists.

Where does the debate go from here? Is the Western mind so locked into its own way of thinking that it cannot assess objectively – or even understand – the way the world looks from any other perspective? And if that is so, what makes it so? Is the collective mind of our culture something we just cannot 'step outside' – however hard we try?

One can drop the word *primitive* from the discussion: it contributes nothing and simply raises tempers. The basic issue is about the limits of the human mind. Does it come in a variety of different versions, as the human body does? Could it be that if your community has a type-A version, there is no way you are going to get on the same mental wavelength as people from a community with the type-B version – and vice versa?

One way out of the white cockatoo impasse is to suppose that there is no God's truth of the matter, and that what your mind allows you to believe – or forbids you to believe – depends on the linguistic equipment with which it is stocked. This relativistic concept of the mind I shall consider further in the next chapter.

Chapter Twenty-Three: The relative mind

Could it be that the way your mind works is dictated by whatever language you have been brought up to speak from birth? If so, that would explain why different communities have different collective minds: they are moulded by speaking different languages: ways of speaking determine ways of thinking.

This theory, sometimes known as 'linguistic relativity', is chiefly associated with the work of two American linguists of the interwar period, Edward Sapir and Benjamin Lee Whorf, although it was suggested much earlier by the German polymath Wilhelm von Humboldt (1769-1859).

According to Whorf, who champions linguistic relativity in what is generally regarded as its 'strongest' version, 'the forms of a person's thoughts are controlled by inexorable laws of pattern of which he is unconscious', and these patterns are nothing but 'the unperceived intricate systematizations of his own language' (Whorf 1942: 252). Thus 'thinking itself is in a language'.

Whorf's claim must not be confused with that of later theorists who postulate a neurological system already present in the brain, on to which any language we learn must be 'mapped'. This system they misleadingly call 'the language of thought' (Fodor 1975), and the argument for it is part of a computational theory of the mind. It runs as follows: in order to learn our first language, we need mental equipment no less complex than that of the structure of the language being learnt. So in order to learn that first language, we must already be in possession of a wordless 'inner' language, or something equivalent: otherwise the learning task would be beyond us. When Whorf spoke of 'thinking in a language', he did not mean any hypothesized system of this kind, but well-known languages like – to take his own examples – English, Sanskrit and Chinese. His thesis is quite the opposite of that held by those who champion 'the language of thought', which is presumably identical for all human beings, being innately installed. For Whorf what mattered were differences between languages.

A simple illustration of these differences would be the problem of translating into French the sentence *She sat down on the chair*. It arises because French has no word corresponding exactly to *chair*. It has a word for chairs with arms and a word for chairs without arms, but no single word which covers all and only chairs, whether having arms or not. What follows from this? It would be absurd to suppose that French speakers are unable to grasp the notion that items of furniture might be classified in a way that simply did not specify whether chairs have arms or not. Nevertheless, it seems reasonable to say that such a classification procedure is not among their usual mental habits, because their native language constantly obliges them to decide whether the particular piece of furniture they are talking about has arms or not; that is, to choose between the French words *chaise* and *fauteuil*. It does not allow them the easy option of forgetting about arms altogether.

This is, admittedly, one rather trivial example of disparity between the vocabularies of different languages, and nothing of world-shaking importance depends on what people say about chairs; but if very many such examples can be found – as they can – one begins to see why Whorf insisted that languages unconsciously impose certain mental habits on their speakers. Such disparities affect not just the classification of everyday objects, but more general aspects of the world, including the supposed properties of time and space, because deciding when and where actions occur is required for describing them. In English one distinguishes between *He is hungry*, *He was hungry* and *He will be hungry*. It makes no sense to say that his hunger was timeless, unless by that is meant that he was hungry all the time. But a language in which verbs were not marked for tense at all would not require that kind of distinction to be drawn. Whorf would maintain that speakers of such a language must have a different concept of time from 'ours'.

If Whorf was right, it seems that the linguistic community of speakers of English must have a different collective mind from that of any linguistic community of non-English speakers.

The attraction of the theory of linguistic relativity is that it seems to explain where otherwise mysterious conceptual differences 'come from'. They are linguistic constructs. It is not that the material world is different as between one community and its neighbours. French furniture is very much like English furniture: so there is no obvious reason why the French should habitually classify furniture without reliance on the concept 'chair', nor, similarly, why the English should do so. It is just that, by historical accident, the vocabularies of the two languages do not coincide in this respect. One language provides a word *chair*, which the other lacks.

Linguistic relativity reverses the usual priority of explanation sought by those who assume that verbal distinctions are simply reflections of distinctions in 'the real world'. For relativists, the mind does not just inspect 'the real world' and construct a conceptual apparatus accordingly, depending on distinctions that 'really' exist out there. (This is *not* to say that followers of Whorf maintain that there are no such things as chairs: the question relates to classification, not to material existence.)

The argument about linguistic relativity provoked a great deal of elaborate and – in my opinion – misguided research, directed towards finding out, for example,

whether speakers from languages with quite different vocabularies of colour terminology 'really did' see colours
differently, or whether speaking a language (like English)
having more than one meaning of a term such as *heavy* 'really did' influence speakers' judgments about the weight
of an object. I call this research 'misguided' because the
proof or disproof of linguistic relativity was never in this
sense an 'empirical question', in spite of the fact that the
jargon favoured by the relativists constantly talked about
different cultures 'seeing the world differently'.

If it is true that the way my mind works is 'strongly'
determined by the language I speak, it ought not to be possible for me to learn a foreign language, once my native
language is firmly in place. But since people apparently do
learn foreign languages as adults, relativists usually shy
away from this conclusion. (They would have to maintain
that the newly acquired language was never properly 'in-
ternalized', but remained as a kind of translation system
superimposed on the language already in place.)

Or else it ought to be true that when I learn a second
language I acquire a second mind. At the very least, the
mind I started out with would now be altered beyond recognition by having to accommodate new systems of classification and expression. Some such 'enrichment' is often
promised by teachers of foreign languages to promote the
educational value of their subject. It seems very dubious.
A more modest conclusion – which I have no difficulty in
accepting – is that learning a foreign language often helps
you to understand issues which would be quite opaque if
you had to rely on English translations for your grasp of
them. And furthermore, that in some cases, without an adequate knowledge of a foreign language, you will unwit-
tingly *misunderstand* those issues. Both in international
politics and in academic studies it happens all the time.

Although Whorfian linguistics is no longer in vogue
with linguists, a distant cousin of linguistic relativity is
still going strong in philosophy of mind, known as 'semantic holism' or sometimes just 'holism'. The basic idea

is that the structure of the human mind ensures that conceptual systems form interrelated wholes, in which one part cannot be altered without affecting the rest. According to Samuel Guttenplan,

> insofar as you think that the meaning of a given sentence in a language depends on its inferential or evidential connections to other sentences in that language, you are a holist about meaning. Or, insofar as you think that, in a given case, the content of someone's belief depends on the inferential or evidential connections to other beliefs that the person holds, you are a holist about content. (Guttenplan 1994: 347)

Taking this at face value, it is difficult to see how anyone could avoid being a holist to some extent, i.e. a part-holist (if that is not a contradiction in terms). No one believes that there are sentences in English that have no connexions at all with any other English sentence, or isolated beliefs that are totally unrelated to any other belief. But few (if any) believe that every sentence in a language is semantically dependent on every other, or that believing in ghosts might be somehow connected with believing that the price of petrol is too high.

Chapter Twenty-Four: The mind defined?

It will seem to many readers rash, or even perverse, to embark on a discussion of the mind without first taking due care to define the words *mind* and *mental*. But so far I have not attempted to define them. Why not?

It is sometimes held that at the frontiers of psychology we find ourselves dealing with indefinables. In Chapter Fifteen I mentioned Susan Greenfield's remark about consciousness: 'We all know what it is, yet it defies definition' (Greenfield 2000: 171). Can the same be said of the mind? Before rushing for this exit, we should pause. Any claim to the effect that 'although-we-all-know-what-X-is-X-defies-definition' is itself puzzling. If we all know what X is, what is the definitional obstacle?

It is interesting that Greenfield does not find any parallel obstacle in the case of other psychological phenomena. She says of memory, for example: 'First, we need to be clear what we mean by the word memory' (Greenfield 2000: 81). She proceeds to say what she thinks a memory is 'for most of us', and goes on to distinguish between short-term and long-term memory, and then to subdivide the latter. There seems to be no definitional impasse. So what exactly is the problem with consciousness?

I suspect that in the case of consciousness – and possibly in the case of memory too – Greenfield is confusing two concepts of definition. What she is looking for and cannot find is not a definition of the word *consciousness* (there are plenty of those available in dictionaries) but something else: what in the philosophical tradition since Socrates has often been called 'real definition': that is, not a definition of a *word* but a definition of the independent *reality* that the word is supposed to designate.

Whether there is any such thing as 'real definition' is a philosophical bone of contention (Harris and Hutton 2007: 37-58). Aristotle thought that it was possible to state what the 'essence' of a thing was; that is, to say what it 'essentially' consisted in. Thus, for instance, to say that a human being is a rational animal would be to give a 'real definition' of the human being (but not of the expression *human being*, which Aristotle could not have defined anyway since he knew no English). The reasons for thinking that the search for real definitions is chasing a will-o'-the-wisp are complex, and cannot be examined in detail here. The best discussion of them is to be found in Chapter VI of Richard Robinson's book *Definition*. But it is worth quoting Robinson's conclusion:

> There is no good in asking 'What is x?', meaning 'What is the thing x?', until the word 'x' means something to us, and means only one thing as opposed to many. There is no sense in saying that 'we don't know what x is' until we do know what the word 'x' means; for, if we did not know what the word 'x' meant, we should be uttering a meaningless noise in saying that 'we don't know what x is'. (Robinson 1954: 192)

The lesson seems to me to apply to Greenfield on consciousness: defining the word *consciousness* must take priority over any inquiry into what consciousness is or might be (if anything at all), because otherwise the inquiry cannot even get started. It is no use trying to sidestep this requirement with the vague assurance that 'we all know' what consciousness is anyway, because it is by no means clear that we do all know, or even agree with one another about what we think we know.

Pretty much the same lesson applies to *mind, mental,* and the whole retinue of terms included in vulgar mind-speak. It is all the more important to bear that lesson in mind when considering the bolder claims currently being made in 'cognitive science'. Igor Aleksander in *How to Build a Mind* maintains not only that the answer to the question 'Can a machine imagine?' is affirmative, but that he and his colleagues are already on the way to designing such a machine (Aleksander 2000). It is clear that the claim is not simply that a machine can do something approximating to what the human imagination can do, but that a machine can have its own imagination. Aleksander believes that building such a machine, or attempting to build one, will throw light on the human imagination and how it works.

For some sceptics, however, attributing any mental powers to a machine betrays either conceptual confusion or a misleading use of figurative language. Nor is it just a question of such claims being unsubstantiated, or factually wrong: they are, it is held, incoherent or meaningless. Even attributing consciousness to the human brain is a 'mercological fallacy'.

> It makes no sense to ascribe psychological predicates (or their negations) to the brain, save metaphorically or metonymically. The resultant combination of words does not say something that is false; rather, it says nothing at all, for it lacks sense. (Bennett and Hacker 2003: 72)

The mereological fallacy is one which involves attributing to parts of a human being (or animal) features and functions that logically belong only to the whole creature.

> Human beings, but not their brains, can be said to be thoughtful or thoughtless; animals, but not their brains, let alone the hemispheres of their brains, can be said to see, hear, smell and taste things; people, but not their brains, can be said to make decisions or to be indecisive.

(Bennett and Hacker 2003: 73)

Bennett and Hacker's mereological argument had been anticipated by Locke in the 17th century. Locke objects vehemently to the notion that the will is free, or is rightly regarded as a free agent. It is you and I who are free, not our wills: 'liberty, which is but a power, belongs only to agents, and cannot be an attribute or modification of the will, which is also but a power' (Locke 1706: II.xxi.14). The question of whether a man's will is free is 'unintelligible' and 'altogether improper': 'it is as insignificant to ask whether a man's will be free, as to ask whether his sleep be swift, or his virtue square'.

All this runs counter to assumptions nowadays made in the field of 'subpersonal psychology', which is overtly based on describing 'subsections of what we normally call persons with the predicates that we typically first learn to apply to persons as wholes' (Leiber 1983). The general argument for subpersonal psychology is made by Patricia Churchland, who claims that what makes sense for one generation does not necessarily make sense for later generations (Churchland 1986: 273-4). New theories bring new terms and new meanings for old terms. That is the way science advances. Furthermore, what it makes sense to say about brains is not restricted by what ordinary lay usage accepts as the customary ways of talking about brains. (The same obviously applies to minds.)

The debate quickly reaches a stalemate, because Bennett and Hacker's response to Churchland's type of argument rests on the prescriptive notion of 'correct' language:

> whether a putative hypothesis makes sense depends upon the meanings – that is, the correct uses – of the words that formulate it. The meanings of words are determined by their rule-governed use, and they are given by what are accepted as correct explanations of meaning by the community of speakers. For explanations of meaning function as rules or standards for the correct use of the

expressions concerned. (Bennett and Hacker 2003: 382)

This will sound all too familiar to those acquainted with the various versions of the language myth that have been formulated from Aristotle down to Saussure and Chomsky. And anyone who has ever done any linguistic fieldwork will find the idea that it is possible to find community-wide consensus about meanings naive. Once the notion that a language is a fixed code, either imposed on or agreed by the entire linguistic community, is called in question, this kind of argument cuts no ice.

What, then, of defining the word *mind*? Why don't I follow Robinson's recommendation and define the word 'x' at the outset? It seems to me that one type of case where Robinson's recommendation cannot be followed is when the use of the word 'x' is itself the contentious issue. I offer no definition because it seems obvious to me that at present there is taking place an interesting debate about how to use this and related words in various developing areas of inquiry. That is one reason for writing this book *now*. For purposes of exposition, as explained at the beginning, I use the word as part of the vocabulary of vulgar mindspeak. But there are clear signs, which it would be foolish to ignore, that this is not the only area of usage relevant to current controversies. To lay down what should be the 'correct' usage of the term, or how the debate should go, seems to me not only foolhardy and pointless but probably counterproductive.

To cite a simple parallel, let me revert to the example I mentioned in Chapter Nineteen. It would now in retrospect look extremely stupid for someone to have argued against Einstein that his definition of *simultaneous* (Einstein 1952 : 21-7) was neither correct nor incorrect but merely senseless. It was certainly incompatible with the Newtonian conception of time, which was itself based upon the 'ordinary language' of timespeak as used in everyday life.

The difference is that subsequent work in science proved that Einstein's redefinition of *simultaneous* was by no means senseless but – for certain purposes – indispensable. We are still waiting, however, for any parallel demonstration in the case of the human mind.

Chapter Twenty-Five: The mind reinstated

Are you by now tempted to give up on mindspeak? Is it riddled with too many traps and deceptions? Might not the best solution be to jettison the whole claptrap of vulgar mindspeak and try starting again from scratch?

I do not think so, even if that solution were possible. But it isn't. It is important to understand why.

We cannot discard mindspeak Locke, stock and barrel, because there is no alternative physical or physiological terminology immediately available to take its place. I cannot, for instance, tell you about one kind of connexion between me and the Battle of Britain except to say that I *remember* it as something I witnessed. I cannot tell you about one kind of connexion between what I am doing now and something I might be doing next week except to say that I *intend* (or do not intend) to do it. To reiterate a point I made earlier, the integration of past, present and future is so fundamental to our understanding of our own lives that 'remembering', 'intending', 'anticipating' and similar matters have to find a place in our language if we are to talk about these things at all.

The primary function of mindspeak is nothing other than to integrate two kinds of experience that we all have: experience of an 'inner' world and experience of an 'outer' world. Philosophers – Wittgenstein prominent among them (Glock 1999: 174-9) – have sometimes been sceptical of this distinction. But it is fairly robust and resistant to scepticism. For I do not have much choice but to regard what is going through my mind at this moment as constituting an activity categorically different from anything you might casually observe me doing (writing, playing the piano, mowing the lawn, etc.). This is not to say that these observable activities are mindless. Their involvement with the mind is something you could ask me about ('Why are you doing this?', 'Do you enjoy it?', 'What do you think it will achieve?' etc.), but how reliable the answers might be is another matter.

Nevertheless, I do not have to produce any 'evidence' for supposing that I have a mind and can think, and can talk about what I think – any more than I have to produce 'evidence' for supposing that at this moment I am sitting at my desk. And anyone who demanded such evidence before taking mindspeak seriously would, in my view, be a victim of profound practical and/or philosophical confusions (as they would if, as I sat at my desk and declared 'I am now sitting at my desk', they said to me 'You have no evidence for that'). As Geach puts it, 'the existence of mental acts [...] ought not to be a matter of controversy' (Geach 1957: 2). I agree. But unfortunately controversy abounds (as Geach goes on to show, adding to it in the process).

In spite of the controversy, however, the fact remains – and it is a fact of first-order experience, not a product of 'theory' – that the conduct of our daily lives constantly *requires* us to distinguish between thinking that something is the case and finding that it *is* – or is not – the case. We sometimes – even often – get it wrong. (I think I have got my wallet with me, but I find I have left it at home.) But if we cannot manage this thinking-it-is-the-case-versus-finding-that-it-is/isn't-the-case distinction *at all*, we are likely to find ourselves in deep trouble with our fellow human beings.

The role of mindspeak in managing this integration between our inner and outer worlds has yet to be studied by linguists in any detail. It remains one of the great tasks for modern linguistics to tackle. Reluctance to tackle it is understandable, because the study bristles with unavoidable difficulties. (It is not even clear to begin with where the boundaries of mindspeak run; for instance, which verbs to include in the class of what some call 'psychological verbs'. Are *see* and *hear* such verbs? I am not sure. The case would have to be argued, whereas no such doubt arises – for me – over *guess* or *imagine*.) But the integrational character of the relationship is undeniable, for a very basic reason. If what we *think* is the case (what is going on in the inner world) never bore any reliable correspondence to what *is* the case (what is going on in the outer world), if our ideas did not match up at all to what was happening in the material environment, then mindspeak would be totally dysfunctional and the human race would never have evolved it as a communicational tool in the first place.

It seems to me important – I would go further and say essential to our humanity – that we have available a language in which verbs like *imagine*, *dream* and *remember* can take the same predicates as *see*, *hear* and *perceive*. (There has to be a parallel between *I imagined him waving a flag* and *I saw him waving a flag*, such that the report of what was imagined and the report of what was seen can be coherently correlated. Without that possibility of correlation between inner and outer worlds, the human being would be a creature of an entirely different kind.)

This primary role of mindspeak has to be distinguished from another role, for which, again, there is no generally recognized term. This is its function in setting a limit to the questions that can sensibly be asked about certain ways of describing our experience. Thus if you tell me 'I imagined him waving a flag', it makes little sense for me to reply 'That's what you say: but be more precise and tell me exactly what neural events occurred in this "imagining"'; for mindspeak resists any further translation into non-mental terms. If you tell me *what* you imagined, that is all I can reasonably ask for (even though I might press you for further imagined details, such as the imagined colour of the flag). Vulgar mindspeak sets its own limits to what can be demanded, just as vulgar bodyspeak does. (If you complain of toothache, I can reasonably ask you 'Which tooth?'; but hardly ask you to identify the neural pathways involved.)

That said, it must be recognized that vulgar mindspeak, while fulfilling both these communicational functions, does not encapsulate some kind of transcendental wisdom about mental activities. It is useful (and essential) as deployed for everyday purposes; but, like all tools, it can be misused. In particular, it can be thoroughly misleading when its distinctions are promoted to the status of theoretical truths. That is exactly what has happened all too frequently in modern discussions of the mind.

So I am not advocating a blind faith in the resources of vulgar mindspeak. As I made clear earlier, I think it harbours the roots of those widespread confusions about human communication that I labelled *the language myth*. By all means, if you wish, speak of 'conveying ideas' to other people; but do not let this expression mislead you into believing that this is what is actually happening when they listen to what you say.

You have been similarly misled if you suppose that since vulgar mindspeak sanctions talk about seeing things 'in the mind's eye', it must be the case that imagining what Julius Caesar looked like involves actually inspecting a private portrait located in one's head. (Exactly this kind of assumption seems commonly to be made in neuroscience: Bennett and Hacker 2003: 180-7). *The mind's eye* is an expression that does no harm, provided it does not dupe people into believing either that human beings have a third eye not externally visible, or that it is another name for the usual binoptic pair when used to focus inwardly.

But when all such caveats have been duly stated, vulgar mindspeak still provides, in my view, the best vocabulary we have for discussing these matters. I cannot see it ever being replaced by a better or more 'scientific' one.

Chapter Twenty-Six: The mind reported

There is a particular type of linguistic device that plays an important role in the way vulgar mindspeak manages to integrate our inner and outer worlds. It was known to grammarians of antiquity as *oratio obliqua* and is nowadays usually called in English 'indirect speech'.

The relation between indirect speech and mindspeak hinges on this. When we pass from *He said: 'Napoleon is dead'* ('direct speech') to *He said that Napoleon was dead* ('indirect speech') it is no longer clear that his exact words are being reported, or even what language he was speaking. So the possibility is open that *He said that Napoleon was dead* is no more than a summary or interpretation, and not a verbatim account. If the former, then a bridge is immediately put in place that allows 'indirect speech' to deliver a report of what was going on in his mind (regardless of whether he actually got round to uttering it or not). So indirect speech lends itself to reporting not just speech, but thoughts, speculations, recollections, intentions, imaginings and all the rest of the tribe of mental acts.

It is because we can make sense in general of the linguistic device of indirect speech that we are induced to believe that *He thought (imagined, supposed, etc.) that such-and-such* is a perfectly valid way of reporting what goes on in the mind. And this in turn makes the mind a far larger theatre to stage possible goings-on than the rather narrow forum afforded by 'reality'. Hence, while we would reject as absurd a report such as 'I heard one of my apple trees telling another to bet on the 2.30 at Exeter', we can hardly quarrel with 'I thought (imagined, dreamt, etc.) one of my apple trees was telling another to bet on the 2.30 at Exeter'.

Now this possibility cannot be dismissed as a kind of marginal aberration of language, because – I suggest – it is the basis of a large part of what we call 'literature'; and the existence of literature is an important component in our grasp of culture, and of ourselves as encultured individuals. In literature we commonly meet omniscient authors who do not hesitate for a moment to tell us about what was going on in the minds of their characters, or even in the minds of historical persons. If we could not make sense of all that, we would have no option but to regard literature as a trivial occupation and our lives would then be impoverished below the level of what I think it is reasonable to regard as human.

When Lady Macbeth cries 'Out, damned spot! Out, I say', we do not doubt that Shakespeare is telling us what she sees in her mind's eye, and that this in turn is the product of her guilty conscience for the crimes in which she has participated. We should otherwise be hard put to it to understand what is supposed to be going on in that scene.

Or, to take a more complicated example, we should be unable to make head or tail of a passage such as the following from Virginia Woolf's *Mrs Dalloway* :

> Her evening dresses hung in the cupboard. Clarissa, plunging her hand into the softness, gently detached the green dress and carried it to the window. She had torn it. Some one had trod on the skirt. She had felt it give at the Embassy party at the top among the folds. By artificial light the green shone, but lost its colour now in the sun. She would mend it. Her maids had too much to do. She would wear it to-night. She would take her silks, her scissors, her – what was it? – her thimble, of course, down into the drawing-room, for she must also write, and see

that things generally were more or less in order.

This is Virginia Woolf deliberately exploiting a technique known to students of literature as 'free indirect discourse', explained in *The Concise Oxford Dictionary of Literary Terms* as:

a manner of presenting the thoughts or utterances of a fictional character as if from that character's point of view by combining grammatical and other features of the character's 'direct speech' with features of the narrator's 'indirect' report. Direct discourse is used in the sentence *She thought, 'I will stay here tomorrow'*, while the equivalent in indirect discourse would be *She thought that she would stay there the next day*. Free indirect style, however, combines the person and tense of indirect discourse ('she would stay') with the indications of time and place appropriate to direct discourse ('here tomorrow'), to form a different kind of sentence: *She would stay here tomorrow*. This form of statement allows a third-person narrative to exploit a first-person point of view, often with a subtle effect of irony, as in the novels of Jane Austen. Since Flaubert's celebrated use of this technique (known in French as *le style indirect libre*) in his novel *Madame Bovary* (1857), it has been widely adopted in modern fiction. (Baldick 1990: 87-8)

But there is much more to it than that. The psychological interest of free indirect discourse, for those who are alert enough to see it, is that it allows for the linguistic integration of inner and outer worlds, and even of divergent points of view in both, in a way that is intuitively recognizable to the reader without authorial explanation. The point here is not the banal observation that Virginia Woolf by means of this technique shows us the situation 'as seen through Clarissa's eyes': that could have been done without resorting to free indirect discourse. The point is rather that *what is seen* through Clarissa's eyes, as reported here by Woolf, does not divide neatly into what was 'really' seen and what was thought, but constitutes an integrated continuum of experience. Furthermore, the reader cannot even distinguish clearly from one phrase to the next whether it is Clarissa or the novelist who is doing the reporting.

This conclusion, doubtless, is likely to be resisted by those philosophers who are stuck in a world where you cannot take a 'what was it' down into the drawing room. The idea of taking a 'what was it' with you – they will insist – just does not 'make sense': there are no such things in reality, there are only e.g. thimbles. Otherwise the universe would be overpopulated with all kinds of shadowy entities threatening to blunt the edge of Occam's razor. This, indeed, is one of the basic difficulties they have with 'the mind': it seems to be a factory not only for making immaterial entities *ad lib*, but for projecting them on to the big screen of the imagination.

There is an even more heretical claim that can be made about free indirect discourse. It runs as follows: reporting our own experiences is always, at least in the first instance, a report in free indirect discourse. For what is called 'free indirect discourse' is nothing more than a formalized (grammatical) recognition of the fact that we do not have minds that insist on categorizing life's components as 'subjective' versus 'objective', or 'personal' versus 'impersonal'.

Philosophers have focussed a great deal of attention on what they call 'first person' reports. The reason is that, according to some, such reports (e.g. 'My tooth aches') have – or can have – an indisputable authenticity, an immunity from error that makes them quite unlike ordinary observational statements about the world. But philosophers have often overlooked the fact that 'It's time for tea' and 'The dustbin needs emptying' are no less 'first-person' than 'My tooth aches', although not in grammatical form. That is to say: we do not usually bother to distinguish carefully between reporting subjective impressions and verified facts, because that is not how we live our lives. It is only in certain types of communication situation and in certain types of cultural context that it matters. Cross-examination in court is an obvious example:

> 'Your statement says that when you left there was no one else in the room.'
> 'Yes.'
> 'How did you know there was no one else in the room?'
> 'I did not see anybody.'
> 'Could there not have been someone sitting in one of the big armchairs on the far side of the room whom you failed to notice?'
> 'I don't think there was.'
> 'You don't *think* so. But you cannot be sure.'
> 'No.'
> 'And yet your statement says the room was empty.'
> 'That was my impression. It appeared to be.'
> 'Ah, your *impression*, you say now.'

As the unfortunate witness squirms in the witness box, we recognize that there, but for the grace of God, go we. In our naivety we take appearances on trust, and hope that our senses are not deceiving us, our memory playing us tricks, or our mind gone on holiday.

Chapter Twenty-Seven: My mind

Finally, 'Do *I* have a mind?' First of all, is the question worth asking? Certainly, because refusing to address it would be tantamount to evading any responsibility for self-understanding. And should the answer be 'no' in my own case, I will have no reason for supposing that anyone else has a mind either. That would be to take a very gloomy view of humanity. It would not be an impossible view, but before taking it I should try to find some very serious arguments pointing in that direction. And I can find none.

So: do I have a mind? Yes, I think so. But I do not believe this on the basis of arguments or 'evidence'. In an earlier chapter I criticized philosophers who seem to suppose that the existence of the mind is proved by our ability to talk to one another. That is not my position. As far as I can see, the ubiquity of linguistic communication in our society is perfectly compatible with the eliminativist view that there is no such thing as the mind.

I think I have a mind, but I also think it unlikely that I shall ever find out much more about it than I can gather from the humdrum experiences of daily life. In particular, I do not think there is much enlightenment to be gained from constructing academic 'theories' of the mind. At least, not if these are constructed in the manner currently fashionable in so-called 'cognitive science'. At bottom, they always turn out to be unverifiable speculation founded on analogies between mind and machine. The machine currently in favour as the model for such speculation is the computer.

The basic reason why these enterprises are vain is that in the mental world there is nothing that corresponds to enhanced observation in the natural sciences. We cannot construct the mental counterparts of telescopes and microscopes. We cannot make microphones to hear the mind talking to itself (if that is what it does). Brain scans can reveal part of what is going on in the cerebral cortex, but a brain scan does not reveal the thoughts of the patient.

Behaviourism stands for me as the paradigm case of what goes wrong when an attempt is made to push traditional 'scientific methods' beyond their intrinsic scope of application. In retrospect, it is perhaps surprising that behaviourism arrived on the historical scene as late as it did. But I take it that the explanation is probably to be found in the deep unacceptability of a mindless universe, both to adherents of traditional religions and to their humanist critics.

There is an irony about the way the behaviourists were subsequently challenged by the 'mentalists'. It resides in the fact that modern mentalism, particularly in psychology and linguistics, is nothing other than behaviourism in a new guise. It does not surprise me that the attack on classical behaviourism was spearheaded by grammarians, because grammarians throughout the Western tradition (an essentially literate tradition) have always started from superficial analyses of strings of words written down, and then explained the 'grammaticality' of these strings as the product of hidden 'rules'. This is the occupational opium of the discipline, and its practitioners cannot do without their daily fix. Behaviourism threatened to deprive them of it and put the study of language on its only true 'scientific' basis, by substituting the study of observable speech behaviour for the armchair postulation of abstract 'rules'.

The grammarians' counterattack consisted not in acknowledging the true character of their enterprise – i.e metalinguistic systematization – but in claiming to be even more 'scientific' than the behaviourists. They did this by a shrewd terminological ploy that cost them nothing: relocating grammatical rules in the brain, but buried somewhere where their 'mental representations' were below the level of consciousness. That left the grammatical fraternity free to carry on as before in the footsteps of their ancestors, postulating ever more complex grammatical systems, and 'explaining' them as the products of invisible 'rules', operating somewhere in the brain, but no one knew where.

It is interesting to reflect that if anyone proposed to study the structure of plants or rocks in the way grammarians now study grammar, they would long ago have been laughed out of the academic court. But because what is supposedly being studied is one aspect of 'the mind' – or, for those who want to hedge their bets, the hybrid 'mind/brain' – few are willing to question it.

The upshot is that modern linguistics has resurrected the traditional language myth and reformulated it algorithmically in computerese. Words are still conveying 'ideas' from one mind/brain to another, in accordance with codes of rules that, unfortunately, prove to lie beyond the reach of consciousness and can only be guessed at. Here we have the counterpart of Freud's claim that however searchingly psychoanalysis trains its searchlight on the unconscious, the ultimate nature of its reality will still remain unknown (Freud 1938: 510). It is the age-old legendary topos of the 'unending quest', now cloaked in scientific respectability.

Now that I have admitted that I believe I have a mind, it remains for me to clarify to my readers what I think that commits me to. First, to clear some possible misconceptions out of the way, I do not think that my mind is my brain (or any part of my brain) under a different description. Nor do I think it is related to my brain as one organ to another. But I do not think it could function without my brain any more than I think I could see without eyes.

It is sometimes argued that although – as experience teaches us – mental activities occur, it is fallacious to infer from this that there actually is a mind *in which* they occur.

In short, the adjective *mental* is all right (when properly used), but the noun *mind* is a trap for the unwary. It suggests a special place or theatre or workshop where mental activities take place. But that – so the argument runs – is the mistake: there does not have to be a mind in which to carry out mental activities, any more than there has to be a garage in which to pump up tyres, lubricate cylinders and carry out other kinds of automobile maintenance. Motorists don't – logically – *need* garages. Thinkers don't – logically – *need* minds.

I see the point of this argument, but I think it is a verbal cop-out; because the way vulgar mindspeak works in practice hardly allows us to admit to mental activities and in the same breath deny that we have minds. I have no ambition to 'reform' vulgar mindspeak, and anyone who has such an agenda I would regard as a quack prescribing linguistic pills for philosophical ills.

So I think I have a mind. But, having said that, I admit that the mind I think I have is largely a linguistic construct. In other words, I can imagine that, if I had been brought up to speak a quite different language, I might have learnt quite different ways of talking about my inner and my outer world – perhaps it might have been a language in which there was no word for *mind* at all. But I think I would have needed *some* way of articulating verbally the connexions and differences between those two worlds.

Some people may object to this talk of 'two worlds'. John Searle condemns it. According to Searle, we don't live in 'a mental world and a physical world' but 'just one world'. Moreover, 'it is the world we all live in' (Searle 2004: 209). I'm afraid that does not correspond at all to my own experience. There is no single, common, undivided world that 'we all' live in. I don't even know who 'we all' are.

What else can I say? It seems to me that to believe I have a body but deny I have a mind is tantamount to denying that I am a person. And to deny that I am a person amounts to refusing to accept what I know about myself:

that I was once a child, that I have grown up, learnt various things, travelled to various places, and that all these experiences are linked by a psychological continuity that makes them mine. This does not mean that I think I am the same person as I was twenty years ago; or that I cannot be mistaken about some of the things I think I did, or some of the things I think are part of the psychological continuum I now identify as mine. But to suppose that *in general* we are deluded about ourselves and all our yesterdays just makes no sense in my language; nor, I suspect, in any other.

The relationship between me, my mind and mindspeak is in some respects clarified by comparison with the relationship between me, my appearance and lookspeak. It makes perfectly good sense for someone to ask for a description of my appearance, and nonsense for me to claim that I don't have one. Anyone can describe how I look. But my appearance is not a physical part of me (like my arms or legs), and it can vary from one occasion to another. So, I think, can my mind, and how it functions in different contexts. Changing your mind is not some kind of metaphor for changes in the brain.

So what do I suppose I have been doing in writing this book and inviting you to read it? First and foremost, I think I have been exercising my own mind. I do *not* think I have been putting ideas into words for conveyance from my mind to yours: that is a mythical enterprise that neither I nor anyone else could engage in. What I am inviting you to do, then, is *not* retrieve and assess the ideas I have carefully encoded.

I hope that, if you have a mind that works like mine, what you will do is read the text and pay attention to the way my discussion is conducted. That will not give you magical access to *my* mind, but it may prompt you to exercise *your* mind in ways I cannot guarantee and cannot even foresee, given that your relevant linguistic experience is bound to be different from mine.

If that happens, it *may* pave the way for a dialogue between us. If you like, you could think of my book as one half of a dialogue, waiting for you to contribute the other half. Dialogue involves the integration of activities on your part and on mine. That integration may prove to be a complete waste of time: or it may turn out to be among the most worthwhile experiences that we could hope for.

Even if what I have written initiates no such dialogue, I am still happy to have written it. As a self-imposed project, it forced me to address certain questions I had previously thought about only vaguely, and obliged me to 'think them through', as one would put it in vulgar mindspeak. And engaging in that kind of enterprise is, for me, one of things it is worth having a mind for, and a language in which to talk about it.

References

Aleksander, I. (2000), *How to Build a Mind*, London, Weidenfeld & Nicolson.

Ayer, A.J. (1950), 'The physical basis of mind'. In P. Laslett (ed.), *The Physical Basis of Mind*, Oxford, Blackwell, pp.70-74.

Baldick, C. (1990), *The Concise Oxford Dictionary of Literary Terms*, Oxford, Oxford University Press.

Balogh, P. (1971), *Freud. A Biographical Introduction*, New York, Scribner.

Bennett, M. and Hacker, P.M.S. (2003), *Philosophical Foundations of Neuroscience*, Oxford, Blackwell.

Blackmore, S. (1999), *The Meme Machine*, Oxford, Oxford University Press.

Bloomfield, L. (1930), 'Linguistics as a science'. Repr. in C.F. Hockett (ed.), *A Leonard Bloomfield Anthology*, abr. edn, Chicago, University of Chicago Press, 1987, pp.149-52.

Bloomfield, L. (1935), *Language*, London, Allen & Unwin.

Bloomfield, L. (1936), 'Language or ideas?'. Repr. in C.F. Hockett (ed.), *A Leonard Bloomfield Anthology*, abr. edn, Chicago, University of Chicago Press, 1987, pp.220-6.

Bruner, J. (1962), 'Introduction' to L.S. Vygotsky, *Thought and Language*, trans. E. Hanfmann and G. Vakar, Cambridge, Mass., MIT Press, pp.v-x.

Butterworth, G.E. (1983), 'Meta-memory'. In R. Harré and R. Lamb (eds), *The Encyclopedic Dictionary of Psychology*, Oxford, Blackwell, p.394.

162

Chalmers, D.J. (1996), *The Conscious Mind. In Search of a Fundamental Theory*, New York, Oxford University Press.

Chomsky, A.N. (1965), *Aspects of the Theory of Syntax*, Cambridge, Mass., MIT Press.

Chomsky, A.N. (1986), *Knowledge of Language*, New York, Praeger.

Churchland, P.S. (1986), *Neurophilosophy: Toward a Unified Science of the Mind/Brain*, Cambridge, Mass., MIT Press.

Churchland, P.M. (1988), *Matter and Consciousness*, rev. edn., Cambridge, Mass., MIT Press.

Clark, A. (2001), *Mindware. An Introduction to the Philosophy of Cognitive Science*, New York, Oxford University Press.

Comte, A. (1844), *Discours sur l'esprit positif*, ed. P. Arbousse-Bastide, Paris, Union générale d'éditions, 1963.

Darwin, C. (1874), *The Descent of Man*, 2nd edn., London, Murray.

Denes, P.B. and Pinson, E.N. (1963), *The Speech Chain*, New York, Bell Telephone Laboratories.

Dennett, D.C. (1987), 'Consciousness'. In R.L. Gregory (ed.), *The Oxford Companion to the Mind*, Oxford, Oxford University Press, pp.160-4.

Dennett, D.C. (1996), *Kinds of Minds. Towards an Understanding of Consciousness*, London, Weidenfeld & Nicolson.

Descartes, R. (1637), *Discours de la méthode*, trans. R. Stoothoff. In *The Philosophical Writings of Descartes*, trans. J.Cottingham, R.Stoothoff and D. Murdoch, Cambridge, Cambridge University Press, 1984-5, vol.1, pp.109-151.

Descartes, R. (1644), *Principia Philosophiae*, trans. J. Cottingham. In *The Philosophical Writings of Descartes*, trans. J. Cottingham, R. Stoothoff and D. Murdoch, Cambridge, Cambridge University Press, 1984-5. vol.1, pp.177-291.

Dixon, N.F. (1987), 'Subliminal perception'. In *The Oxford Companion to the Mind*, ed. R.W. Gregory, Oxford, Oxford University Press, pp.752-5.

Einstein, A. (1952), *Relativity. The Special and the General Theory*, trans. R.W. Lawson, 15th edn, New York, Crown.

Fodor, J.A. (1975), *The Language of Thought*, New York, Crowell.

Freud, S. (1938), *The Basic Writings of Sigmund Freud*, trans. A.A. Brill, New York, Random House. Repr. 1995.

Freud, S. (1949), *An Outline of Psycho-Analysis*, trans. J. Strachey, London, Hogarth.

Geach, P. (1957), *Mental Acts. Their Content and their Objects*, London, Routledge & Kegan Paul.

Glock, H-J. (1999), *A Wittgenstein Dictionary*, Oxford, Blackwell.

Greenfield, S. (2000), *Brain Story*, London, BBC Worldwide.

Gregory, R.L. (1981), *Mind in Science*, London, Weidenfeld & Nicolson.

Gregory, R.L. (1987), 'In defence of artificial intelligence – a reply to John Searle'. In C. Blakemore and S. Greenfield (eds), *Mindwaves*, Oxford, Blackwell, pp.235-44.

Guttenplan, S. (1994), 'Holism'. In S. Guttenplan (ed.), *A Companion to the Philosophy of Mind*, Oxford, Blackwell, p.347.

Harris, R. and Hutton, C. (2007), *Definition in Theory and Practice*, London, Continuum.

Hampshire, S. (1971), 'Critical review of *The Concept of Mind*'. In O.P. Wood and G. Pitcher (eds), *Ryle*, London, Macmillan, pp.17-44.

Hobbes, T. (1651), *Leviathan*, ed. C.B. Macpherson, Harmondsworth, Penguin, 1968.

Hofstadter, D. (2007), *I Am a Strange Loop*, New York, Basic.

James, W. (1904) 'Does "consciousness" exist?', *Journal of Philosophy, Psychology and Scientific Method* 1.

Jespersen, O. (1922), *Language. Its Nature, Development and Origin*, London, Allen & Unwin.

Kenny, A.J.P. (1973), 'The origin of the soul'. In Kenny, A.J.P., Longuet-Higgins, H.C., Lucas, J.R. and Waddington, C.H., *The Development of Mind. The Gifford Lectures 1972/3*, Edinburgh, Edinburgh University Press, pp.46-60.

164

Kenyon, F. (1941), *The Myth of the Mind*, London, Watts.

Kim, J. (2006), *Philosophy of Mind*, 2nd edn, Cambridge, Mass., Westview.

Kirk, G.S., Raven, J.E. and Schofield, M. (1983), *The Pre-Socratic Philosophers*, 2nd edn, Cambridge, Cambridge University Press.

Kirk, R. (2005), *Zombies and Consciousness*, Oxford, Clarendon.

Lacan, J. (1949), 'Le stade du miroir comme formateur de la fonction du Je'. Repr. in J. Lacan, *Écrits*, vol.1, Paris, Seuil, 1966, pp.89-97.

Lakoff, R. (1975), *Language and Woman's Place*, New York, Harper & Row.

Leiber, J. (1983), 'Subpersonal psychology'. In *The Encyclopedic Dictionary of Psychology*, ed. R. Harré and R. Lamb, Oxford, Blackwell, pp.618-9.

Levelt, W.J.M. (1981), 'The speaker's linearization problem'. In H.C. Longuet-Higgins, J. Lyons and D.E. Broadbent (eds), *The Psychological Mechanisms of Language*, London, Royal Society / British Academy, pp.91-100.

Lévy-Bruhl, L. (1910), *How Natives Think*, trans. L.A. Clare, ed. C.S. Littleton, Princeton, Princeton University Press, 1985.

Lienhardt, G. (1966), *Social Anthropology*, 2nd edn, Oxford, Oxford University Press.

Locke, J. (1706), *An Essay Concerning Human Understanding*, 6th edn. London, ed. A.C. Fraser, 1894, Repr. New York, Dover, 1969.

Luria, A.R. (1968), *The Mind of a Mnemonist*, trans. L. Solataroff, New York, Basic.

MacKay, D.M. (1987), 'Determinism and free will'. In Gregory, R.L. (ed.), *The Oxford Companion to the Mind*, Oxford, Oxford University Press, pp.190-2.

McGinn, C. (2004), *Consciousness and its Objects*, Oxford, Clarendon.

Matilal, B.K. (1990), *The Word and the World*, Oxford, Oxford University Press.

Moore, G.E. (1912), *Ethics*, London, Oxford University Press.

Moulton, W.G. (1970), *A Linguistic Guide to Language Learning*, 2nd edn, Modern Language Association of America.

Nagel, T. (1974), 'What is it like to be a bat?', *Philosophical Review*, 83, 435-50.

Nathan, P.W. (1987), 'Nervous system'. In Gregory, R.L. (ed.), *The Oxford Companion to the Mind*, Oxford, Oxford University Press, pp.514-34.

Oswald, I. (1987), 'Dreaming'. In Gregory, R.L. (ed.), *The Oxford Companion to the Mind*, Oxford, Oxford University Press, pp.201-3.

Paley, W. (1802), *Natural Theology. Evidences of the Existence and Attributes of the Deity Collected from the Appearances of Nature*, London, Faulder.

Palma, A. (2004), 'Automaticity', *Language Sciences*, 26 (6), 609-19.

Papineau, D. (2000), *Introducing Consciousness*, Cambridge, Icon.

Pinker, S. (1999), *Words and Rules*, London, Weidenfeld & Nicolson.

Plato, *Complete Works*, ed. J.M. Cooper, Indianapolis, Hackett, 1997.

Pribram, K.H. (1971), *Languages of the Brain*, Englewood Cliffs, Prentice-Hall.

Robinson, R. (1954), *Definition*, Oxford, Clarendon.

Rose, D. (2006), *Consciousness. Philosophical, Psychological and Neural Theories*, Oxford, Oxford University Press.

Rosenthal, D. (2005), *Consciousness and Mind*, Oxford, Clarendon.

Russell, B.A.W. (1912), *The Problems of Philosophy*, London, Oxford University Press.

Russell, B.A.W. (1927), *An Outline of Philosophy*, London, Allen & Unwin.

Ryle, G. (1949), *The Concept of Mind*, London, Hutchinson. Page references are to the reprint in Penguin University Books, Harmondsworth, 1973.

Sacks, O. (1965), *The Man Who Mistook His Wife for a Hat*, London, Duckworth.

166

Saussure, F. de (1922), *Cours de linguistique générale*, 2nd edn, trans. W. Baskin, New York, Philosophical Library, 1959.

Savage-Rumbaugh, S., Shanker, S.G. and Taylor, T.J. (1998), *Apes, Language and the Human Mind*, New York, Oxford University Press.

Schaller, S. (1991), *A Man Without Words*, New York, Summit.

Searle, J.R. (1989), *Minds, Brains and Science. The 1984 Reith Lectures*, London, Penguin.

Searle, J.R. (1997), *The Mystery of Consciousness*, London, Granta.

Searle, J.R. (2004), *Mind. A Brief Introduction*, New York, Oxford University Press.

Shaffer, J. (1967), 'Mind-body problem', *The Encyclopedia of Philosophy*, ed. P. Edwards, New York, Macmillan, 5, 336-46.

Skinner, B.F. (1987), 'Skinner on behaviourism'. In Gregory, R.L. (ed), *The Oxford Companion to the Mind*, ed. R.L. Gregory, Oxford, Oxford University Press, pp.74-5.

Spender, D. (1980), *Man Made Language*, London, Routledge & Kegan Paul.

Sutton, J. (2004), 'Representation, levels and context in integrational linguistics and distributed cognition', *Language Sciences* 26: 503-24.

Swann, J., Deumert, A., Lillis, T. and Mesthrie, R. (eds) (2004), *A Dictionary of Sociolinguistics*, Edinburgh, Edinburgh University Press.

Tammet, D. (2006), *Born on a Blue Day*, London, Hodder & Stoughton.

Tannen, D. (1990), *You Just Don't Understand*, New York, Morrow.

Trench, R.C. (1851), *On the Study of Words*. Repr. London, Dent, 1927.

Turing, A.M. (1950), 'Computing machinery and intelligence', *Mind*, vol. 59, no. 236. Reprinted in A.R. Anderson (ed.), *Minds and Machines*, Englewood Cliffs, Prentice-Hall, 1964, pp. 4-30.

Velmans, M. (2000), *Understanding Consciousness*, London, Routledge.

Vygotsky, L. (1962), *Thought and Language*, trans. E. Hanfmann and G. Vakar, Cambridge, Mass., MIT Press.

Wallace, A.R. (1903), *Man's Place in the Universe. A Study of the Results of Scientific Research in Relation to the Unity or Plurality of Worlds*, London, Chapman & Hall.

Watson, J.B. (1924), *Behaviorism*, People's Institute Publishing Co. Page references are to the reprint in the Norton Library, New York, 1970.

Weiskrantz, L. (1986), *Blindsight*, Oxford, Oxford University Press.

Whorf, B.L. (1942), 'Language, mind and reality'. In B.L. Whorf, *Language, Thought and Reality*, ed. J.B. Carroll, Cambridge, Mass., MIT Press, 1956, pp.246-70.

Wiedemann, T.E.J. (1996), 'Barbarian'. In S. Hornblower and A. Spawforth (eds), *The Oxford Classical Dictionary*, 3rd edn, Oxford, Oxford University Press, p. 233.

Young, J.Z. (1986), *Philosophy and the Brain*, Oxford, Oxford University Press.

Index

Abstraction, 99, 106, 110
Akrasia, 25. *See also* Free
  will.
Aleksander, I., 141
Anaxagoras, 116-18
Animism, 15
Anthropology, 125,
  127-31
Archetypes 82. *See* Jung
  C.J.
Argument from design,
  115-16
Aristotle, 25-6, 49, 121-2,
  140, 143
Artificial intelligence. *See*
  Machines
Austen, J., 151. *See also*
  Speech
Aycr, A.J., 64

Baldick, C., 151
Balogh, P., 81
Behaviourism, 13-17, 39,
  51, 105, 156-7
Bennett, M., 4, 84, 88-9,
  93, 141-3, 148

Berkeley, G., 19
Bhartrhari, 45
Blackmore, S., 85
Blindsight. *See under*
  Consciousness
Bloomfield, L., 14-15, 51
Boswell, J., 19
Brains, 7-10, 47, 49-50,
  61-3, 81, 141-2
Bruner, J., 103
Butterworth, G.E., 92

Causation, 17, 27-8, 82,
  118
Chalmers, D.J., 3, 115
Child prodigies, 97
Chinese room. *See under*
  Searle, J.R.
Chomsky, A.N., 15, 82,
  143
Christianity, 122
Churchland, P.M., 62
Churchland, P.S., 142
Clark, A., 4, 85
Codes. *See under* Gram-
  mar

Cognitive science, 31, 63, 88, 141, 155
Cognobabble, 4, 16, 130
Collective mind, 5, 121-5, 133-5; and Jung, C.G., 82
Colour-blindness, 22
Communication, 50, 58-9, 69-70, 103-4, 109-12, 124. *See also* Telementation
Computers. *See* Machines
Comte, A., 128
Connectionism, 41
Consciousness, 13-14, 79-89, 101, 139-40; blindsight and, 83-4; self-consciousness 91-5
Creationism, 116
Cudworth, R., 115

Darwin, C., 115-16, 127-9
Definitions, 3, 55-6, 64, 69, 89, 139-44
Denes, P.B., 52
Dennett, D.C., 67-70, 86
Descartes, R., 7-11, 20, 31-2, 35, 37-9, 103
Determinism, 26, 28
Deumert, A., 125
Dictionaries. *See* Mind: mental dictionaries
Dixon, N.F., 83
DNA (deoxyribonucleic acid), 40, 53
Dreams, 89

Einstein, A., 112-13, 143

Eliminative materialism, 62, 155
Essences, 140
Ethics, 26
Ethnocentricity, 127
Euphemism, 125

Fatalism, 26
Feminism. *See* Language, feminism
Flaubert, G., 151
Fodor, J.A., 133
Folklore, 13
Folk psychology, 4
Forster, E.M., 26
Free indirect discourse. *See under* Speech
Free will, 25, 83, 142
Freud, S., 79-82, 103, 157

Geach, P., 73-6, 146
Genius, 97
Glock, H-J., 145
Grammar, 49, 61, 70; codes, 38-41, 50, 52-3, 57-8, 73, 159; grammaticality, 100, 103, 156-7; rules of, 33, 40, 82, 142, 156-7. *See also* Chomsky, A. N.; Dennett, D. C.; Saussure, F. de; Vygotsky, L. S.
Greenfield, S., 83, 86, 89, 91, 139-40
Gregory, R.L., 10, 80, 116
Guttenplan, S., 137

Hacker, P.M.S., 4, 84, 88-9, 93-4, 141-3, 148
Hampshire, S., 2
Harris, R., 140
Herodotus, 121
Hobbes, T., 44-5
Hofstadter, D., 19
Holism, 136-7
Homunculus fallacy, 46-7
Higher Order Thought (HOT), 59, 95. *See also* Telementation
Humboldt, W. von, 133
Hutton, C.M., 140
Hylozoism, 115
Hypnosis, 97

Idealism, 19
Identity theory, 8
Integration, 76, 109-13, 145-7, 149, 151-2, 160
Interactionism, 82
Invariants, 57

James, W., 27
Jespersen, O., 123
Johnson, S., 19
Jung, C.G., 82

Kenny, A.J.P., 76
Kenyon, F., 61
Kim, J., 22, 70, 87-8, 130
Kirk, G.S., 117
Kirk, R., 17, 32
Knowledge by acquaintance, 92-3

Lacan, J., 91, 94

Lakoff, R., 123
Language, 33-9, 51-2, 68-71, 93-5; feminism and, 123-5; linguistic relativity and, 133-7; universals and, 75
Language myth, 38-40, 46-52, 55-9, 73-7, 79-82
Leiber, J., 142
Levelt, W.J.M., 45
Lévy-Bruhl, L., 129-31
Lienhardt, G., 127
Lillis, T., 125
Linguistic relativity. *See under* Language
Linguistics, 15-16, 49, 51, 80, 146-7, 156-7
Literacy, 45-6, 111, 156. *See also* Writing
Literature, 150-1
Locke, J., 55-6, 142
Logic. *See* Reasoning
Logos, 121-2
Luria, A.R., 98

Machines, 7-10, 64, 76, 141; minds as computer, 31-5, 133, 155-6
MacKay, D.M., 28
Matilal, B.K., 45
McGinn, C., 89, 93
Mental. *See* Mind
Mind: acts or activities of, 9, 44, 73, 124, 148-9, 157-8; capacities of, 10, 75, 128-9, 141-2;

Mind (*continued*)
  cosmic, 5, 115-19;
  discourse and, 44;
  distributed cognition
  and, 63; facts (or con-
  cepts) of, 49; habits of,
  134; mental dictionaries
  of, 50-1, 61; mentalism
  and, 15-16, 55, 103,
  156; mentality of 121;
  mental reality and, 16;
  mind/body problem, 1,
  7-9; other minds,
  19-23; primitive mind,
  127-31; processes of,
  44, 82; representations
  of 16, 157; states of,
  17, 25, 44, 59, 62, 77,
  88; traits of, 123; units
  of, 51
Mereological fallacy,
  141-2
Mesthrie, R., 125
Meta-memory, 91
Mezzofanti, G.C., 97
Moore, G.E., 26, 28
Moulton, W.G., 52
Mozart, W.A., 97

Nagel, T., 87
Nathan, P.W., 62
Necessity of identities,
  130-1
Neuroscience, 40, 84, 88,
  98-9, 148
Neutral monism, 8
Newton, I., 112
Nous, 117-19

Oratio obliqua. See
  Speech, indirect
Ordinary language, 3, 143

Paley, W., 115-16
Palma, A., 62
Panpsychism, 115
Papineau, D., 87
Pinker, S., 50
Pinson, E.N., 52
Plato, 43, 45, 80, 118-19
Political correctness, 125,
  127
Prelogicality. *See under*
  Reasoning
Pribram, K.H., 53
Psychoanalysis, 82, 157

Qualia, 22-3, 87

Racism, 127
Raven, J.E., 117
Reasoning, 7, 69, 80; pre-
  logicality and, 129-31
Relativity, 113
Robinson, R., 140, 143
Rose, D., 17, 41, 47, 84
Rosenthal, D., 3, 59, 77,
  95
Rules. *See under* Gram-
  mar

Rushdie, S., 21
Russell, B.A.W., 27, 92-3
Ryle, G., 9-11, 27, 62-3

Sacks, O., 98-9
Sapir, E., 133

Saussure, F. de, 49-52, 104, 106, 143
Savage-Rumbaugh, S., 70
Schaller, S., 101
Schofield, M., 117
Searle, J.R., 3, 31, 86, 115, 158; chinese room and, 33-5, 39-40
Semantic holism. *See* Holism
Shaffer, J., 8
Shakespeare, W., 49, 150
Shanker, S.G., 70
Signs, 37-9, 51, 101, 104
Simplicius, 117
Skinner, B.F., 14
Sociology, 128
Socrates, 25, 43-4, 46, 118-19, 140
Solipsism, 19
Speech, 43-51, 80; free indirect discourse, 151-2; indirect speech, 149; inner speech, 43, 45-7, 104-6; speech signal, 15; telementation and, 38
Spender, D., 123-4
Subliminal perception. *See* Consciousness, blindsight and
Sutton, J., 63
Swann, J., 125

Tammet, D., 99-100
Tannen, D., 124
Taylor, T.J., 70
Telementation, 37,

50, 109; Higher Order Thought (HOT) and, 59; thought transfer ence, 37, 55; Vygotsky L and, 103. *See also* Communication; Grammar, codes; Language myth
Telepathy, 37, 116
Trench, R.C., 122-4
Turing, A., 32, 34

Velmans, M., 62, 85-6
Vulgar mindspeak, 2-5, 8-14, 37-9, 61-4, 79-80, 145-9
Vygotsky, L.S., 103-6

Wallace, A.R., 115
Watson, J.B., 13-15, 37-9
Weiskrantz, L., 83
Whorf, B.L., 133-6
Wiedemann, T.E.J., 121-2
Wittgenstein, L., 145
Woolf, V., 150-2
Writing, 38, 43, 45-6, 111. *See also* Literacy

Young, J.Z., 40